Marketing
Management

CASES FOR CREATIVE PROBLEM SOLVING

Laurence Martin Weinstein
Sacred Heart University

Madan Annavarjula, Ph.D.
Sacred Heart University

South-Western College Publishing
Thomson Learning™

Australia • Canada • Mexico • Singapore • Spain • United Kingdom • United States

Creative Problem Solving Cases for Marketing and Management
by Dr. Laurence Weinstein and Dr. Madan Annavarjula

Publisher: Dave Shaut
Aquisitions Editor: Pamela M. Person
Developmental Editor: Mardell Toomey
Executive Marketing Manager: Steve Scoble
Production Editor: Kelly Keeler
Manufacturing Coordinator: Sandee Milewski
Production House: Cover to Cover Publishing, Inc.
Printer: Mazer Corp.

Printed in the United States of America
1 2 3 4 5 03 02 01 00

For more information contact South-Western College Publishing, 5101 Madison Road, Cincinnati, Ohio, 45227 or find us on the Internet at http://www.swcollege.com

For permission to use material from this text or product, contact us by

• **telephone: 1-800-730-2214**
• **fax: 1-800-730-2215**
• **web: http://www.thomsonrights.com**

Library of Congress Cataloging-in-Publication Data
Weinstein, Laurence,
    Creative problem-solving cases for marketing and management / Laurence Weinstein
    and Madan Annavarjula.
        p. cm.
    ISBN 0-332-40273-70
        1. Marketing--Decision making--Case studies. 2. Marketing--Management--Case
    studies. I. Annavarjula, Madan, 1960- II. Title.

HF5415.135.W44 2000
658.8'02--dc21

00-027888

This book is printed on acid-free paper.

DEDICATION

To Ellie, Tanya, Josh and Seth, Mom and Lynn

To Shoba, Deevena, and Mom

Contents

Four partners start up a tapas bar and gourmet food restaurant in New Jersey next to a large state-funded university. Their marketing challenge is to establish the restaurant and reach financial break-even before their investment funds run out.

Key Topics: Market segmentation, business start-up, obtaining and building consumer awareness product life cycle.

A British-owned supermarket chain is faced with growing domestic competition and the threat of Wal-Mart taking over the lion share of business in the food industry.

Key Topics: Strategic planning, competitive analysis, organizational response to external threats, test marketing, initial foray into at-home shopping over the Internet.

An executive responsible for recommending investment opportunities in an organization that provides the food industry with advice on how to market private label goods must make a critical choice affecting the firm's international strategic plan.

Key Topics: Assessing overseas markets, evaluating risk, strategic planning, assumptions regarding the ability of organizations to take their know-how and use it effectively in different cultural and business settings.

A product manager uses observational qualitative research to help inform herself about a potentially devastating problem that could sink her newest product launch.

Key Topics: New product development, packaging, consumer research, quantitative analysis, crisis management.

The director of a clinic needs to find a way to determine if her organization should change its strategic plan in order to remain financially viable.

Key Topics: Strategic planning, positioning, consumer focus group qualitative research, risk management.

Key Topics: Market segmentation, packaging, positioning, strategic planning and analysis.

SECTION NINE   INTERNET MARKETING AND ECOMMERCE   161

Preface

We are very pleased to present to you an exciting new case book created expressly for the purpose of promoting more creative problem-solving opportunities for students in the classroom. With over 30 years of college undergraduate and graduate teaching experience between us, we know these cases work and how helpful they are to students' learning experience. While preparing these cases, we have interviewed managers, entrepreneurs and executives. We explored their environments and motivations, carefully analyzed their positions and options in order to put together original and compelling case studies. We feel sure these will engender intense involvement and discussion for both students and instructors. Interesting and challenging *real life problems* are important for engaging student's interest as they learn about business theories and practices. Even more important, however, are the problem-solving *skills they will acquire* which are so vital to their success as they enter today's demanding and changing business environment.

All of the cases provide memorable learning experiences because they are . . .

- "classroom-tested"
- understandable without requiring complex math calculations
- brief but comprehensive
- designed for courses related to both marketing and management
- adaptable for role-play
- suitable for various teaching purposes and for addressing multiple concepts
- a mixture of short and somewhat longer cases, qualitative and quantitative emphasis and variety of subject matter
- easy to use—table of contents shows the major topics addressed by each case study

We believe our book is unique because we share a perception that creativity as a problem-solving tool in marketing and management classes is somewhat undernourished—not by design, but perhaps through mere lack of attention by some text and case writers. Therefore, we have included what we feel are important cases requiring careful thought and analysis.

Our cases are intentionally versatile. Consider, for example, the "Arbor Fabrication and Manufacturing Company" case study. On one level, the case deals with the allocation of resources in an industrial marketing environment. The case offers much more, however, if the instructor wishes to take the case to a higher level: there was a gender clash between the majority stake female owner and her "junior" male partner; there was a lack of strategic vision and planning and the case can also be examined in an entrepreneurial context because of the challenges and rigors facing bootstrap operations.

All cases have theoretical underpinnings that are discussed fully in the **Instructor's Manual (ISBN 0-324-05977-9)**. As active instructors, we know how important it is to create strong instructional material for our colleagues. We consider the instructor's manual to be an integral part of the package and have worked very carefully to make this supplement thoughtful, thorough and helpful. We have devoted equal or greater time to the instructor's manual as we have to the cases themselves.

Please let us know your experiences with the cases we have presented in this casebook. Also, two of the entrepreneurs whose experience we used in several cases are hoping to receive feedback from you and/or your students. Skip Dickerson, owner of the web site, Provincetown.com, and Phil Johnson, CEO of Innovative Therapists International, decided to work closely with us specifically because they are looking for insights and suggestions on how to improve their internet businesses. These are real people with real problems that require solutions. We hope interaction with them will be beneficial for both these company owners as well as students.

Acknowledgements

The authors would like to acknowledge and thank the following people:

- Dean Benoit Boyer, College of Business, Sacred Heart University, for his support of our research efforts.

- Dr. B. Elango, Assistant Professor, Illinois State University, for his help in writing the Technically Mediated Instruction case study and for his help in preparing the Instructor's Manual.

- Dr. Sri Beldona, Vice President Strategic Planning, Marketing Management Inc., for his help in writing the Private Label Marketing case study.

- Mr. Georges Hilbert for his draft of the Tesco, plc case study which was edited and revised by the
- casebook authors.

- Dr. Theresa Madonna for her input to the West Coast Family Planning case study.

- Mr. Diego Arias-Carballo for his help with the Breakfast in Europe case study.

Due to issues of confidentiality, we cannot mention those who gave us important company information and insights which that led to many of our case studies. Even though these people cannot be recognized by name, we are indebted to them and wish to express our deep appreciation for the time and effort they so selflessly offered so that every case study in this book is rooted in actual events, companies and people.

Note that cases which have disguised names, events and data are indicated by an asterisk appearing on the first page of the case.

SECTION ONE
Overview of Marketing, Business Ethics

Introduction

Seated around a kitchen table, David Beliva, Horace Graham, and Sandy Shoemaker were attempting to figure out what to do next with their new product concept, a portable study carrel that could be moved from classroom to classroom or within a library setting to accommodate changing space needs around exam periods. Study carrels themselves were not a new product idea; what the three entrepreneurs had done was develop a lighter, very mobile study desk that would also permit the user to change an educational setting with very little physical effort in the classroom.

Possible applications to business settings were also anticipated down the road.

Company Background

The company, "Technically Mediated Instruction," was formed a few years ago by three neighbors who lived in Oakland, California, a sprawling city just across the bay from San Francisco. The three men were all fairly new to the neighborhood and had recently met at an outdoor block party barbecue.

After reviewing the current state of the baseball penant races, the weather, and how they felt about the high cost of living in California, they went on to discuss their jobs. David was a public elementary school teacher, Horace was a sales representative for a national publishing company, and Sandy was a manufacturing supervisor in charge of quality control for a consumer goods producer located nearby.

Trading "war stories" about their work environments, David mentioned he was particularly upset as a teacher because several of his students every year were just not able to concentrate and learn in his classroom. He had tried various techniques using all the latest learning theories. Every classroom in the building now had several computers linked to the Internet to help students focus their attention on the task at hand, but a few students remained easily distracted and David found they could not deal very successfully with the general noise level and commotion found in a typically busy and bustling sixth grade inner city classroom.

Stimulated by David's intensity, Horace and Sandy felt they wanted to hear more from David about how he might solve his problem with children who could have learning problems. One thing led to

---

* This case was written by Dr. Laurence Weinstein and Dr. B. Elango, who is currently at Illinois State University. All information in the case is disguised.

another and soon the three neighbors were really getting into how to help David with children who were born with, or somehow acquired, attention deficit disorder or learning disabilities that prevented the children from progressing in a "typical classroom."

Started as simply a friendly exercise to work with David and his frustrations as a teacher, the three budding entrepreneurs soon realized they were getting more and more serious about developing some type of product that could offer real benefits to both teachers and librarians: a portable study desk, or carrel, that could provide students with a desk or work space with folding sides and legs. Students with learning issues could still be a part of the classroom, but now they could also have an opportunity to work without the distractions of seeing their classmates around them.

Their discussions expanded to include libraries. In a library environment, the carrels represented a different use entirely: they could be set up when overloads around examination times depleted the library's resources of more expensive and permanent study desks. This would give the library administration added flexibility without creating a large storage problem during slack periods nor would it involve spending a lot of money.

Horace, who said he was constantly asked to attend company-sponsored seminars and conferences, believed for-profit and not-for-profit organizations could also benefit from mobile study carrels in their human resource departments. "David, a lot of people don't realize how much education is going on now within corporations. We may actually train and educate more adults than universitites do around the United States. A portable study carrel could also have some value to company learning centers as well."

Moving Ahead

The three men formed Technically Mediated Instruction, incorporated themselves with the help of a local lawyer, and then set out to find a manufacturer who would be willing to build a prototype portable study carrel. Sandy had a contact just outside of San Carlos, California, and in discussing the details of the project with the vice-president of manufacturing for the firm, Sandy convinced him to build 10 prototypes to TMI's specifications at a reduced rate of only $15 per unit. All three partners were too busy to travel to the actual manufacturing location, but Sandy assured his friends that everything would work out fine. Sandy believed he had developed a nice rapport with the manufacturer and everything seemed under control.

Three months later, the completed carrel prototypes arrived at Sandy's home via United Parcel Service, just as his contact at the San Carlos firm had promised they would.

Promotional Materials

In the meantime, David had approached a creative team working at BBDO Advertising Agency out of San Francisco. The team, comprised of a senior copy writer and art director, were asked to help TMI develop promotional materials for the carrel that would be used first to attract attention to the product, second to stimulate teacher and librarian interest, and finally, to generate orders.

There was advertising copy to be written and a brochure to be developed that would be mailed to various school-based buying departments once the company's advertising began in educational magazines and journals. The print ad copy would include an address and toll-free telephone number for those readers interested in further details about the TMI carrels. The brochures would include an order form and a list of prices for different size carrels and also accessories that could be purchased along with the portable desks.

In order to integrate the prototype production with the advertising and brochure development, the three entrepreneurs came up with their own version of a Gantt Chart:

Schedule of Major Activities April—October

	April	May	June	July	August	September	October
Order prototypes	X						
Receive prototypes		X					
Create ad copy			X				
Create brochures					X		
Place advertising						X	X

The Commitment Is Made

The actual carrel prototype production and shipment expenses would only amount to roughly $200. Far more important were the creative fees for the copy writer and art director, the advertising space, and the brochure printing. The last three activities would cost in excess of $20,000. After discussing the financial commitment with his family, each partner took the money out of savings or borrowed his share, and a company bank account was started after a Federal identification number was obtained. After almost a year of planning and strategizing, now it was finally for real. TMI was "born."

The three partners were elated when the carrel prototypes were delivered since advertising for the product would break within 60 days, but they noticed right away that the manufacturer had made several changes in the physical product without first consulting with TMI. The changes turned out to be significant.

Upset, Sandy called his contact at the firm and asked why materials had been substituted for the ones they had originally specified for the carrel. The response was that the company could not meet TMI's cost targets with the lighter aluminum Sandy had asked for. Instead, heavier but less expensive steel had been used. Further, instead of side walls made of plastic, the walls were put together with compressed wood composite. Unfortunately, both these substitutions had substantially increased the weight of the portable carrels. David was extremely concerned. "If our customers cannot lift this carrel easily and move it around without fearing some type of physical injury, we can forget it. Our whole product benefit of light weight and mobility will be gone."

It's Too Late!

By this time, however, the advertising space had been ordered and paid for. Since TMI was a new advertising account, the magazines had insisted on payment with the orders. Worse, the brochures had all been printed with price lists dated for that fall. Additionally, Horace and Sandy had already planned to attend an upcoming educational products trade show in Chicago and take three vacation days from work. The partners decided they had no choice but to hope for the best because the carrels that had been shipped to them were the very carrels they needed to start showing to prospective school teachers and librarians, as well as bring to the Chicago show.

The First Orders

The advertising campaign was officially launched that fall right on time, and within three days of the company's first magazine insertion, orders started to come in to TMI from at least five states. Elated and excited, Sandy called the manufacturer and asked that 100 carrels be produced immediately and direct-shipped so as to avoid back orders. The TMI partners did not want to frustrate their carrel buyers with an extended wait period while TMI searched for a more amenable manufacturer or until their current manufacturing source came up with the proper materials to make the carrels as light as possible. David in particular felt vindicated with this initial wave of orders because it confirmed his belief that mobile, lightweight carrels would be in great demand from the education industry.

Just four weeks later, things did not look as exciting for TMI.

"Trouble In Paradise"

A letter arrived from a teacher in Harrisburg, Pennsylvania. She explained how she had ordered the study carrel for herself for use in her own apartment since her three children all seemed to have trouble concentrating on their homework at night. This part of the letter excited David as he read it. The three partners had never considered a home market for the study carrel at all, but this teacher evidently had understood the benefits of home use of the carrel as soon as she had seen TMI's advertisement. "High fives" for her!

David read on. "Even though I think your carrel concept is a good one, I wish to return the product I purchased from you because I find it too heavy and awkward to set up for my young children. I have a history of back trouble and the carrel is simply too heavy for me to take from the closet and move it into the living room. Do you have another model that is lighter while still being sturdy?"

David surmised the company was in trouble.   It seemed from the woman's letter the mobility of the study carrel had been seriously compromised. The product was not providing the benefits they had intended. Horace and Sandy called from Chicago.

They were coming home to California and wanted to meet with David. They were bringing with them some negative comments from the Chicago show concerning the carrels. Horace said, "It's going to be a long evening ahead for all of us, David. . . ."

Case 1.2
The Young Account Executive

The Air . . .

. . . was so thick with tension, I felt it was hard for me to breathe right. I had trouble swallowing. It was all so sudden, so unexpected. Ron, my supervisor, was glowering at me. I mean, the guy was really upset. And since he was my boss at Rumrill-Hoyt Advertising, that meant I was going to be upset. I just didn't know about what.

That would change in a hurry.

I Had Earned . . .

. . . my AB degree in Economics from a small, co-ed liberal college in Maine just four years before starting as an Account Executive at the ad agency. Now college life seemed far away. Since graduation, I had earned my MBA degree from a big city university and then gone on to start my marketing career at a large consumer packaged goods manufacturer located in Ohio.

My two-year excursion to the midwest was used as a stepping stone to land a plum account executive position with a mid-size advertising agency in New York City that also had an office in Rochester, New York, to service its Kodak client. Moving from a multinational corporation to the advertising agency had been a culture shock, but I got used to it soon enough. The biggest change was not having someone, somewhere within a company with thousands of employees worldwide to help me with any task that came across my desk, from researching and choosing consumer premiums, to figuring out 18-month rolling production schedules. Now, at Rumrill-Hoyt, I depended on "me, myself, and I" for answers.

I was given my own office and employed by what I took to be a young, hungry advertising agency, which, to its credit, had plunked down the bucks to rent a fancy address on Madison Avenue in New York City. My salary was better than $100,000 annually, and I had a very liberal expense account. What more could a 26-year-old ask for?

My First Travel Assignment . . .

. . . didn't seem so bad. It wasn't exactly glamorous, either, since it was a trip to Baltimore, but the city had really tried to change its image by rescuing the waterfront from terminal decay. I thought I might even take in a game at Camden Yards if the Orioles baseball team were playing during my trip.

The purpose for my three days' absence from the office was to conduct some store checks for one of my clients' brands over at American Home Products. We didn't have any of their major national products, but we were told if we did a bang-up job on several of their smaller brands, the agency would be given a shot at something far bigger. That motivated all of us to work extra hard on everything we did for AHP.

Rather than use a limousine to get to the airport, I asked my wife to take me to LaGuardia Airport. We lived in the Bronx at the time right across from Van Courtland Park, so the trip to the airport usually took no more than 30 minutes if we didn't hit traffic travelling into Queens. I had asked the advertising agency's travel booking service to find something modestly priced for my hotel stay near the airport. Staying near the airport always seemed to make sense to me because picking up and returning the rental car and getting into and out of the city would be easier and quicker.

I Knew ...

... senior management ordered Lincolns or even the fancy 4 × 4s for themselves when they went on the road. Being a junior account executive, I just asked the travel group to order me up a standard Ford Contour or the Pontiac equivalent. For three days I could live with just about anything that came with four wheels as long as it had air conditioning. I didn't care about color, style, leather, or bucket seats— just air conditioning during the summertime in sweltering Baltimore, Maryland.

Food was eaten whenever I could take a quick break from the store checks I was conducting among several national supermarket and drug store chains. It was never anything fancy, just enough carbohydrates and protein to get me through the day.

The three days passed quickly. I store checked my legs silly and came back with results from more than 35 Baltimore-area stores. Careful to keep good notes, I figured I could impress my supervisor, Ron Ghermack (disguised), with in-depth analyses about how our AHP accounts were doing. I had carefully noted shelf facings by product size and brand for our accounts and the competitors.

I had taken down pricing information, any out-of-stocks I saw, in-store promotional activity, free-standing floor displays, and any other point-of-purchase information I thought relevant. This was going to be one heck of a report and something Ron could show management with pride, then the AHP client. I had received terrific training at how to conduct store checks at my first job and I felt it was going to solidify my career at Rumrill-Hoyt right from the beginning.

I Handed in ...

... my expense account without giving it much thought. It was pretty much straightforward. With no clients to entertain, and since I traveled alone, there wasn't much to it. The airline flight had been billed directly to the advertising agency so I only had five entries:

Expense Item	$ Amount
Three nights, hotel stay	$252.10
Car rental, corp. discount	102.75
Limousine ride, one way only	35.00
Food	95.00
Miscellaneous	15.50
Total	**$500.35**

I sent it off to the Accounting Department and promptly forgot about it. The financial folks were pretty good about travel reimbursements. You could figure they would have a check in your hands within 72 hours after they received the reimbursement request. No problem.

I was wrong. Oh, I got my check all right. It was the "no problem" I was wrong about.

Ron's Face Was Getting Red . . .

. . . as he started to talk to me. "Close the door!" he ordered and I meekly went to close his office door. I couldn't imagine what I had done wrong.

My site visit reports from the Baltimore trip had been completed the day before. I felt in my gut I had hit a home run. Ron seemed really pleased with the hard work and thoughtful analysis I had put into the store checks when he skimmed my work. It was just a matter of time before one of the senior management people came over to me and offered me congratulations. Sure, it wasn't as good as a pay raise or promotion, but you could keep track of these minor successes and eventually they would add up to something big.

However, Ron wasn't handing out any kudos today.

"Are you trying to make the rest of us look like the southbound end of a northbound mule?" he started. I figured it was a pretty clever way to start dumping on me. Nice touch. Humorous, but the point was made.

I offered, "Ron, I don't have a clue what you're talking about. Can you explain why you're so angry?"

"Yeah, kid, I'll explain it. Actually it's very simple. You submitted an expense account report for Baltimore that barely cleared $500 and you were there for three days."

Okay, I thought quickly, guilty as charged. That's what I spent. That's what I submitted. Am I missing something really big here?

Ron continued. "Look, I've been to Baltimore for the agency, just like you. I've been to D.C., Atlanta, Boston, Philadelphia, and other cities up and down the East Coast. Not just once to each city, but multiple trips just to help get information for clients. So, too, have a dozen other account executives from this office. And you just made us all look bad."

I was stammering. "How, Ron? I put in eight-, nine-hour days and site visited about 35 retail outlets. What did I do wrong?"

Ron looked at me incredulously. "You don't know? *You don't know?*" His voice was rising sharply as he spoke to me. "You stayed in Baltimore for 72 hours and all you spent was $500 to get there and back, not counting the flight? You must have forgotten something. Clients you entertained. Dinners you didn't include. Perhaps a night at the hotel that didn't get added in. Lots of things. You figure it out."

I thought desperately about what I could have forgotten. I sat thinking while Ron patiently waited for me to say something. What should I say? "Ron, I'm sorry," I finally blurted out, "But I can't think of anything I left out. My wife drove me to the airport. I could put in the tolls and travel reimbursement for the car mileage. Yeah, I forgot to put that in."

Ron retorted, "I'm not discussing petty ante amounts of money here. I'm not talking about $10 or $20. I'm talking about $300 to $500 that's 'missing' from your expense report. No one has ever been on the road to Baltimore or D.C. or Atlanta and not spent close to $1,000 while away for three days. You go on your first trip for the advertising agency and come back spending just half that amount. Everyone over in Accounting, if they all got to see your expense voucher, would want to know how come you could travel to Baltimore and back for just $500 when all the rest of us spend twice that amount. Routinely."

I was too surprised to say anything. Surprised? No, I was stunned. I had made a major mistake and I hadn't even been with the advertising agency for two months. "Well, Ron, what do I do now? I mean, I handed in my expense account already."

Ron actually smiled at that point and some of his testiness seemed to dissipate. "One of my contacts over in Accounting saw your expense account and questioned the disparity between your expenses on this trip and everyone else's who's been there for the past several years. Luckily, I was able to get your expense voucher back from Accounting before too many eyes got to see it. Do you realize how embarrassing it would have been if the voucher had gotten to the office of the Director of Financial Services? We all would have been asked to explain why you could go and come back from your trip for half of what we always put in for."

I could feel my heart rate starting to come down. Okay, some person over in Accounting had kept the wrath of God from coming down around my ears. Now it seemed all I had to do was deal with Ron. But what exactly was I supposed to do next?

Since Ron appeared to have gained control over his emotions, I ventured, "So what do you want me to do with my expense report?"

"Don't you understand by now?" he responded.

"Well, since I seemed to have made a mess of it the first time, why don't you make it absolutely crystal clear to me?"

Ron's face wasn't friendly and neither was his tone. "Okay, here's what you have to do. You have to 'remember' that you spent at least $300 more in Baltimore. Is that so difficult? Why do I have to spell it all out for you? You're supposed to be smart. MBA and all that stuff. Are you suddenly dense?"

I was responding as if on automatic pilot. "Change my expense report? That's what you want me to do? Even though I only spent $500, you want me to report at least $800 in expenses because everyone else regularly requests at least $800 for their three-day stays? But I didn't spend $800 and that means you're asking me to falsify the report." I tried to remain calm but I could feel a sense of impending dread coming over me.

Ron had been looking at some paperwork on his desk while I was speaking. He didn't look up. "Change it. Submit it to me within the hour. Take the extra money and put it towards your Roth IRA for all I care. And from now on, you will submit all your expense requests to me first. Now get to it."

I left Ron's office and went into my own office, closing the door. I felt sick. Nothing I had learned at college or "B school" had prepared me for this moment.

SECTION TWO
Market Positioning and Segmentation

Dismay

A recent American visitor to central Europe was dismayed to see very few of her favorite cereals in the Alima supermarket around the corner from her rented apartment. The store was located in the downtown area of Luxembourg City and it offered about 15 varieties of breakfast cereals compared to typically 50 or more in an average U.S. supermarket.

Surprised by the lack of choices among the breakfast cereals, the visitor turned to a European friend and exclaimed, "What you do folks do for breakfast over here? I can't believe you have such a poor cereal selection from which to choose!"

Nonplused, her friend replied, "The breakfast cereals you're referring to in our grocery stores are stocked mostly for the American and Canadian tourists who come here or those North Americans who come and work in our country before moving on. In Europe, we have never had the tradition of eating cereal and milk for breakfast. Instead we have fresh breads or croissants with jams and jellies along with coffee."

Chastened, the American visitor knew she had no choice but to change her meal habits and tastes while in Europe. However, she secretly wished that Kellogg's, General Mills, and Quaker Foods would help change the breakfast culture in the European Union nations. It certainly would make it easier to visit or work there!

Visits to Other Stores

Not quite ready to give up, the American visitor also went to the Match, Cactus, and Auchan supermarket chains; the results were virtually the same. Few cereal brands were found, and very little space given over to the cereal category. Clearly, the next six weeks visiting Europe were going to be a bit of a challenge, at least for breakfast! (A planogram of the Alima cereal section can be found in Table 1.)

The general impression of the cereal category was that:

1. Most cereal boxes were small, roughly a U.S. 13-oz. box size.

2. Most brands had one facing, only a few had two or more. A store visit to a Cactus supermarket back in 1996 showed Kellogg's with 24 total brand facings compared to Nestle's/General Mills with only 3. The subsequent visit in May 1999, suggested Nestle's and G.M. were making some inroads against Kellogg's.

3. Cereal seemed expensive. The 500-gram boxes appeared to offer a relatively better value per gram, but prices were high across the board compared to U.S. cereal prices.

4. Few recognizable brands were offered to North American shoppers.

5. The cereal section was almost an after-thought with units stocked on the *lower* half of the shelf. The top part of the shelf was allocated to baby food!

6. The entire length of the cereal offerings was roughly four meters (12–13 feet). Compared to a typical U.S. supermarket, cereals in Europe were virtually invisible to the casual consumer. One had to consciously look for it while pushing one's cart through the circuitous aisles.

7. No promotional activity was evident on the packages.

Joining Forces

Kellogg's, headquartered in Battle Creek, Michigan, has long had a foothold in Europe and probably should be credited with introducing American-style breakfast cereals to the European continent. The General Mills Corporation ("G.M."), with headquarters in Minneapolis, Minnesota, and the Nestle Company, located in Zurich, Switzerland, joined forces in 1997 as a consortium to challenge Kellogg's for supremacy on store shelves within the European Union. G.M. had the cereal manufacturing know-how and existing successful brands to put on the table; by venturing with Nestle, G.M. immediately acquired marketing intelligence and distribution strength that otherwise could have taken years to acquire. Top marketing executives at G.M. announced they were about to wage a war against Kellogg's for the heart, mind, and stomach of European consumers. The winner would be generating sales in the millions of pounds, francs, marks, and pasetas for years to come.

But, Did It Really Matter?

However much bravado the G.M. and Nestle's team exuded over their battle with Kellogg's, the American visitor was left wondering. Did it really matter who won and who lost? After all, the European consumer appeared to have a disinclination to buy American-style cereals. Why would the war waged over a comparatively small amount of shelf space matter to the average European shopper? S/he probably could care less who won and what brands were being stocked. The marketing challenge seemed to be whether anyone could get the European breakfast eater to switch their current eating habits and begin to consume cereal in the morning.

Mulling It Over

While evaluating the decision of General Mills and Nestle's to form their consortium and to try to get a toehold against Kellogg's, one would have to ask: Was it possible for consumers to change their breakfast habits? The answer, at least for the United States, was "yes."

After all, cereal for breakfast was a fairly "new" phenomenon. Prior to the 20th century, typical U.S. breakfasts consisted of meat, eggs, and bread. In the belief that the diet of the American consumer could be upgraded considerably from this high-fat menu, Dr. R. B. Kellogg formulated and began to market his own breakfast cereal product back in 1922. It took a decade to catch on, but when it did, people young and old realized the value breakfast cereal had. It was healthier, easier to prepare, and less expensive than meat.

Patience, good, healthy products, and thoughtful promotional programs aimed at educating Americans as to the value of cereals all paid off. Today, the breakfast cereal market in the United States is estimated at over $1.5 billion annually.

Could this not be duplicated in Europe as well?

Kellogg's Brands

	Rice Krispies	Fruit & Fiber	All Bran	Country Store
Grams	375	375	500	750
U.S. $	$3.03	$3.17	$3.44	$4.78

Nestle's + General Mills

	Cluster	Kix	Nesquik	Apple Minis	Chocapic	Fitness
Grams	375	375	375	375	375	375
U.S. $	$3.17	$3.00	$3.00	$3.00	$3.00	$3.17

Dr. Oetker's Weetabix Brands   Alima—Private Label

	Vitalis	Weetos	Frutibix	Grano Vita	Alima
Grams	375	375	500	500	375
U.S. $	$2.22	$3.17	$3.42	$3.50	$2.00

Note: One ounce is roughly 28 grams. A box of Rice Krispies with 375 grams is equivalent to a small, 13-oz. box of cereal in the United States.

Table 1. Store Planogram, Cereal Section, Alima [*]

---

[*] Planogram data were generated by Diego Arias-Carballo.

Bad News

The Vice-President of External Affairs knocked on Lauren Desay's office door and asked to come in. "Sure!" Lauren replied with a smile, "Come on in and make yourself at home."

Sue Albrite sat across from Lauren and looked gloomy. "You're not going to believe this, but your recommendation to the Board to begin using the name of the museum as a 'brand identity'—much like for-profit companies do with brands such as Tide or Pepsi Cola or MTV—has been rejected."

"They turned it down? Why on earth would they do that? " Lauren exclaimed.

Sue sighed, "Well, that's hard to fathom, but I think it's because they don't trust the concept of 'marketing' the museum. Aggressive marketing would somehow 'cheapen' our image around the Cincinnati area, according to this view. Also, they don't really understand the value of 'branding' within the context of a not-for-profit organization. They think it's something corporate America would do, but not an educational organization like ours."

Background

The Otis Museum was founded in 1920 by former public school teachers in a residential area located in the northern edge of the city. The motivation behind the museum's founding was to encourage children and their parents to have access to hands-on exhibits through visual arts and historical representations. It was the first major attempt to create such an institution in the city, especially with a hands-on approach to its exhibits and activities. Previous to this, most scientific and educational exhibits for children were focused on artifacts with young people limited to making dioramas of historical events. The Children's Museum in Brooklyn, New York, had pioneered this new hands-on museum concept for young people at the turn of the 20th century followed soon after by the Children's Museum of Boston.

Roughly 500,000 visitors came to the museum each year with a total of 60,000 square feet of space. A bit more than half of that was used for actual exhibitions; the remainder was used for storing exhibitions and executive offices for the 110 staff members.

The museum had a $6.5 million annual operating budget. Revenues were derived from ticket sales, donations, sponsorships, and grants. About one-third of all guests were subsidized by the museum

---

* All information in the case including the name of the museum is disguised.

with some attendees coming in for free as part of the museum's mission to serve the whole community without regard to ability to pay.

The three core areas of the museum were the visitor area, historical research and presentations occurring both in and outside the museum, and a visual arts school where area residents could attend workshops and classes. The staff prided itself on providing accurate and interesting materials for children, adults, and amateur and professional academic researchers.

Organizational Structure

The Otis Museum was organized using a functional or departmental approach:

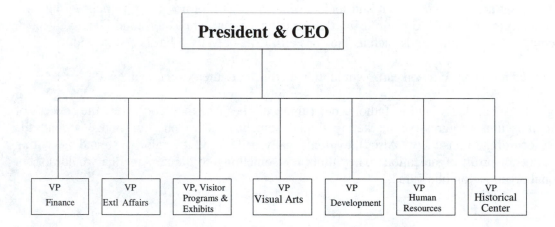

Lauren Desay, in her position as Marketing Manager, reported to the Vice-President of External Affairs as did a manager for public relations. External Affairs was responsible primarily for cultivating corporate sponsorships and for developing better relationships with city and community leaders. All departmental vice-presidents and the director of the Historical Center reported directly to the president and CEO. Of the 110 museum staff members, 35 were considered managers.

Target Audience

The target audience for the Otis Museum was families with children 2–10 who lived near the museum itself, and suburban families who were willing to drive in from outlying areas to the downtown location. This meant having bifurcated demographics with urban users tending to come from lower income families of color and/or recent immigrants, and suburban children who came from white, higher income families. Head Start, Cincinnati public school kindergartens, and neighborhood organizations were important feeder groups for the museum.

Competition

Compared to other museums across the country, the Otis Museum was a much smaller operation. However, with close to a half-million visitors annually, the museum provided an important educational outlet for young, largely urban children. The hands-on approach to museum exhibits had become popular, however, in the region, and the museum faced competition from similarly themed exhibitions in the midwest.

Television and increasingly computers and the Internet vied for people's attention. With family discretionary time becoming more scarce as entertainment and educational options increased, the staff at the Otis Museum knew they had to compete in a crowded marketplace of ideas and activities directed to young people.

Media Expenditures

Lauren was responsible for placing $50,000 annually of print advertising announcing new exhibits in local newspapers. She also edited the four-page museum newsletter, inserted six times each year in *The Cincinnati Family's Paper*, a free publication reaching 60,000 area homes. Another 40,000 newsletters were distributed to visitors, museum members, donors, and community organizations like the YMCA.

No radio or television broadcast advertising was currently being used, but Lauren was starting to obtain free mentions for the museum from several radio stations by agreeing to provide free visitor passes. These passes were used as part of promotions sponsored by paying clients. The clients were pleased to be associated with the museum. The station was glad to get the paying clients. And Lauren was getting the museum mentioned on-air at virtually no incremental expense because she was giving away passes that represented only an "opportunity cost" to her organization.

Competitive Advantages

The Otis Museum held several key advantages over some of its closest geographical rivals in the hands-on category of exhibitors. First was size. This meant having more exhibits of interest to a wider range of people, regardless of age. Second, the museum had the funding power to mount larger and better exhibits than most other competitors in the region. Third, the museum's focus was always on multiculturalism; this mission of serving urban populations made it distinctly different from suburban counterparts. Fourth, the museum had an active gift shop whose goal was to be on par with the quality products available from commercial enterprises such as LearningSmith and Noodle Kadoodle.

The most successful exhibit for the museum to date was the summer of 1999 presentation of "Blue and Grey," an exploration of American Civil War history through art, artifacts, and mixed media. Although the purpose of the exhibit was serious, the presentation did include live re-enactments with the opportunity for local area residents to dress up in period costumes. The event was considered a big success.

The newest exhibit in the museum allowed children and their parents to explore different artistic designs and approaches, art tools, and a variety of artistic expression. Another exhibit displayed the different communities that made up greater Cincinnati and was funded by a local real estate company that received an official "co-sponsorship" of the event. The publicity announcements released by the museum all prominently mentioned the name of the real estate firm. This marked the first time in the museum's existence that an exhibit had been named after a co-sponsor and reflected the marketing staff's belief that corporate tie-ins were becoming increasingly necessary to attract sponsorship money.

The Problems

Every enterprise faced challenges and the Otis Museum was no exception. Foremost in the minds of everyone on the staff was the issue of transportation and accessibility for visitors. Although the museum was located just three blocks from the central bus station, its geographical setting in downtown Cincinnati created the perception the museum was hard to reach because of the often congested streets surrounding the museum, especially during the morning and evening commutes.

Urban families at times felt the three-block walk from the bus station was difficult given the need for the youngest children to be put in strollers or baby carriages that were hard to navigate on busy city streets. Suburban families believed anything near the central city was simply not worth the driving and parking hassle and expense. Another issue was perceptual. Since suburban families were more likely to become members and thus help the museum financially, the staff needed to cater to their needs while remembering that the museum's stated mission was to direct its energies to urban users.

However, these very same urban families complained occasionally they did not feel welcome at the museum, and their stated position was that the staff were concentrating too much on pleasing the suburban visitors due to their higher incomes.

This indicated another weakness: a lack of customer sensitivity and adequate training among the staff who tended to be affluent suburbanites themselves. An unresolved issue asked by some staff members was what exactly the museum should be attempting to do for the local community and what the experience should be for each visitor. There were many interpretations among the staff on how to answer those questions, but no comprehensive, overall vision or customer satisfaction statement truly provided direction.

For instance, was the Otis Museum supposed to dedicate more of its staff efforts to its membership or spread those efforts and attention around equally to every visitor? Was the immediate surrounding urban community supposed to be given a higher priority or not? To what degree was the institution driven by a multicultural mission? Was the focus to be on children, young adults, parents, or researchers? Were school tour groups to be given priority over individual visiting families? Should the museum seek traveling exhibits or use only those events the staff generated internally?

A problem directly related to Lauren Desay's work was her belief the museum did not have a cohesive identity among its target audience members or its corporate sponsors. Prospective visitors did not appear to have a clear idea of what the museum offered and why it was worth seeing. The new president and CEO had worked hard to get the organization to re-dedicate itself to its urban-focused mission. However, museum-sponsored research showed that this effort had not been communicated very well to the public. Additionally, it was unclear to what extent the paying attendees wanted—or needed—to know about these efforts in order to be convinced to visit more frequently.

Finally, and perhaps most crucially, as a service provider rather than a marketer of a tangible good, the museum offered an array of experiences to visitors that could greatly affect their perception of the museum, but which the museum's staff was not evaluating or attempting to upgrade. One of the great untapped opportunities, Lauren believed, was for the museum's top management group to decide how best to create a set of experiences that truly reflected the museum's stated mission. This might affect even mundane tools like the central automatic voice messaging system, food provided in the small cafeteria, and other visitor amenities. "The museum's managers need to consider," Lauren said, "that the museum offers a myriad of experiences that we should be thinking about more proactively and managing much more carefully than we actually do today."

Available Research

Research Associates had conducted research "pro bono" for the museum using visitor intercepts, focus groups, and staff interviews. Their conclusions were that the museum had been providing the community with very mixed messages about what the museum stood for and offered to its target audience. There was a high emotional affinity towards the museum from regular visitors, but a lack of coordination among departments. It seemed there was a haphazard approach to marketing the museum that had led to a situation where no one, clear message was getting out about what made the museum worth visiting for prospective attendees.

The Museum's Response

To correct this problem, the president established a Task Force on Branding that had the charge of developing a plan to coordinate and clarify all of the communication vehicles used by the museum to reach its public. Due to negative staff feelings about the word "branding" (too commercial, too marketing-oriented), the task force name was changed recently to the Task Force on Identity Development so that the word "branding" would not get in the way of the group's goals.

Lauren Desay, in her position as Marketing Manager, had urged the task force to establish guidelines and policies on how the name, logo, visuals, and other physical manifestations of the "Otis Museum of Cincinnati" should all be coordinated and have a similar look. She added, "If all of our literature, brochures, teaching materials, and letterhead start relating visually to each other, we can begin to develop a consistent look. The museum has the opportunity to treat its unique designation, 'The Otis Museum of Cincinnati' as a brand name just as Xerox, Exxon, Beatrice Foods, and Unilever have brand names for their products."

Lauren felt the museum's board and some of its "old blood" staff members did not appreciate the value of using a marketing orientation. If anything, she believed the museum acted more like a production-oriented enterprise, racing to create each new exhibit. Real constraints on time and budget limitations made it difficult to pay attention to customer feedback either before ("pre-testing") or after ("post-testing") exhibitions were presented. At least "managing the brand" would introduce some valuable marketing techniques that could help the museum's management group.

Several members of the task force did not share Lauren's point of view. Their arguments included these points:

1. We've been open to the public for more than 85 years. So far the museum has done quite well without branding and using other such marketing techniques. Why change now?

2. Forcing communications to all have the same "look" would take away the creativity and independence of the different departments. It would make External Affairs much too invasive in the creative process and interfere with each department's ability to decide for itself how best to reach the public.

3. What works for commercial enterprises around branding is not meant to be used by a not-for-profit organization. Our mission is far different than IBM or Microsoft.

Despite these misgivings, Lauren believed she could make her case with the task force and, ultimately, to the board of trustees. With her background in cable television marketing in Minneapolis, Lauren felt she could convince enough staff members, and then the board, to begin an effective effort at treating the museum more like a marketing entity.

After Sue Albrite's visit, Lauren was a bit dejected and concerned. Branding was such an accepted part of marketing managers in private industry. Why couldn't she use this same concept for the museum?

Case 2.3
The Polaris Café:
Attracting and Retaining a Loyal Customer Base*

A Time of Joy

Ben Reynolds, one of four partners in a new gourmet restaurant venture formed as a limited liability corporation located in New Brunswick, New Jersey, was waiting impatiently until the day's edition of the *Newark Star Ledger* was delivered to newsstands at 5 a.m. Eagerly, Ben and his three business associates, Kyle Roman, Sid Carter, and Dominick Trioli, raced through the paper until they got to the entertainment section. They knew the paper would contain a review of their restaurant, the Polaris Café.

They all collectively held their breaths as they turned to the food page of the *Ledger*. Ben saw it first, exclaiming, "They gave us three stars!" For the paper's 100,000+ readers, that meant the Polaris Café had just received a priceless recommendation from the food editor: the restaurant that had opened just four months ago on March 1 was rated as a "very good" dining experience by the paper's restaurant reviewer.

Exhaling slowly, the partners looked around at each other and then screamed and shouted their joy, their relief, and their unabated excitement at receiving this important public affirmation. Months of hard work and a personal financial commitment among the partners, which had now exceeded half a million dollars just to open the restaurant, seemed about to pay off.

Background

Ben Reynolds first met Kyle Roman 15 years ago when both of them were involved in the music scene in and around New Brunswick. Home to Rutgers University and such corporate giants as Johnson & Johnson, the city's town government had been trying for years to pull the city out of its economic doldrums since the 1970s.

Ben was a health care professional who, in his spare time, was a member of an alternative band. Kyle loved music, too, but his "day job" consisted of owning and operating several bookstores in central Jersey and an art gallery in New Brunswick. Kyle invited Ben to come to his gallery to see the featured artists, but as they met and approached the gallery they realized something was terribly wrong. The entire building housing the gallery was on fire, threatening to engulf everything in its path.

Later, Ben said, "You can't imagine what it was like to be that close to terrific heat and flame. We were like crazy people trying to save all of the artwork. I didn't know Kyle very well then, but going

---

* All information in the case including the name of the restaurant is disguised.

in and out of that building while it was on fire was quite a bonding experience for us. We've been very close ever since . . . and we saved all of the artwork!"

That friendship led to Kyle asking Ben in 1998 to join him with two other business associates, Sid and Dominick, to help them start a new restaurant. Kyle was the overall manager of the project because of his previous successful retail experience. Sid was to be in charge of the financial aspects of the venture including attracting investor money and handling bank loans. Dominick, whose parents had started and were still running Timothy's, a restaurant landmark in New Brunswick, was to be in charge of payroll and purchasing. Ben was tapped to be in charge of marketing and public relations.

Choosing a Theme

New Brunswick boasted a lot of different types of restaurants and "watering holes," some catering to the huge student population at Rutgers University while others targeted the professional and managerial, white-collar population. Students had a wide variety of bars from which to choose, and the restaurants they favored tended to price their entrees from $5–$12.00. Upscale restaurants—such as Stage Left and The Frog and the Peach—that had received four-star ratings from area newspapers, priced their entrees from $17.50 on up.

Positioning their restaurant and selecting a format would be one of the first and most critical decisions the partners would have to make. Kyle and Ben had both traveled to Europe separately, but recently they had toured Italy and Spain together. They were impressed by what they saw—and ate. In addition, both knew the entertainment scene in New York City (located some 35 miles away) quite well and what was considered "trendy" and "hot" in the restaurant category. Together, after much discussion, informal research, and negotiation among themselves, the four partners decided to open a restaurant that featured a tapas bar along with a fine dining section so that they could capture both the student population and upscale professionals.

Tapas

Ben explained tapas by saying, "If you've never been to Spain, you've missed out on one of the most interesting and fun culinary happenings in Europe. Spain is filled with tapas bars; they are places you can go for liquid refreshments while enjoying inexpensive appetizers called 'tapas.' Tapas can be made of vegetables, meat, or fish and are usually priced from a few dollars to perhaps $10.00 tops."

Selecting the Site

Once the theme had been chosen, the next task was to find a suitable retail location for the restaurant. This took months of work, but the partners were able to achieve a breakthrough when they found out that Johnson & Johnson was knocking down a building near the theatre section of the city to build more office space. The first floor was to be dedicated to retail; once this information became available the partners pounced. They signed a long-term lease, putting them in the heart of New Brunswick and a rebuilding program that eventually would include a convention center, mall, movie theatres, and four blocks of modernized brownstones. Importantly, with three car parking decks on the drawing boards, one of the worst aspects of driving into a downtown area would not be much of a problem for future visitors to the city.

The Name

"Polaris Café" was selected as the restaurant's name because Polaris, the North Star, has been used for centuries as a major navigation aid and guiding light for travelers who sought out new and exciting destinations. The partners were hopeful the name of their new venture would be perceived as another interesting destination to seek out and enjoy for those people who lived and/or worked in central New Jersey.

Restaurant Description

The tapas bar area featured a Mediterranean influence on the colors, walls, wood floor, and choice of tables and chairs for the room. Kyle was in charge of the architectural plans and he decided to include a 30' mahogany bar for the room along with candles on each table, wrought iron candleholders on two walls, floor-to-ceiling clear glass windows facing onto the street for the other two walls. Seating capacity was roughly 100 diners for the room that measured about 1,200 square feet. The goal was to create an environment that would seem to be like the Soho or West (Greenwich) Village areas of nearby New York City. It would have New York style without the high prices and would be a bit more casual. Music piped in through a sophisticated stereo system included jazz, flamenco, and Latin sounds.

Since Kyle and Ben had an interest in—and had carefully studied—both the wine and beer beverage categories, they decided to add further value to the restaurant by offering 100 different types of wines from which customers could choose a vintage either by the glass or bottle. They invested in and set up two "wine keepers"; each wine keeper re-pressurized opened wine bottles to keep the remaining wine fresh for the next customer.

In addition, the café was planning on creating an outdoor section off of the tapas bar during summer months where an additional 30 diners could be served. The outdoor space was approximately 400 square feet. Combined, the indoor and outdoor tapas section of the café added up to about 1,600 square feet and could accommodate 140 people. The remaining 400 square feet of space was turned into a fine dining room for up to 60 patrons with an entirely different motif and theme.

This fine dining area, located behind the mahogany bar, featured gourmet food and had carpeted floors, unusual artwork and tapestries on the walls, and more of a quiet, romantic setting than the front of the restaurant. The menu was changed about every two months to reflect new dishes and normal product turnover depending upon what customers said they liked and disliked. A mixture of meat, fish, and vegetarian meals were on the menu.

Target Audience

Ben planned on advertising the restaurant in selected major area newspapers and magazines. Although his promotion budget was modest, Ben believed it would be sufficient to get the local community initially interested in the café. Trial was critical; if people could be stimulated to come to the café and try its food, Ben was sure they would become repeat customers.

The two key market segments for Polaris to attract were the older undergraduate and graduate students who were looking for a more sophisticated place to go to eat without draining their entertainment budget. This audience typically sat in the tapas room, rarely venturing into the more formal dining area. The latter attracted older patrons who had more income, and who typically worked in a managerial or professional position in the community.

Pricing

Tapas were priced from $4 to $9 a piece, which meant college or graduate students could eat at the Polaris Café for about $10 each if they included wine and/or beer with their light meal. Desserts were priced in the range of $5–$7 each. Free cheese tastings were available to motivate prospective diners to come to the tapas bar. This was a bit more expensive than many of the other restaurants that sought out the student dollar, but the unique nature of the tapas bar was expected to draw in the curious and differentiating younger clientele.

In the fine dining section, entrees ranged from $15 to $23. As the menu was a la carte, an individual having a complete meal with wine could expect to pay $30 and up for their meal. However, this still compared favorably to the two nearby four-star restaurants where a typical meal could easily cost $75 per person.

In this fashion, the partners felt they had carefully selected food and price strategies that would put them in a niche by themselves. The tapas bar was an important point of distinction for Polaris; an equally important set of decisions allowed the tapas bar and fine dining section to remain reasonably priced and very competitive with other nearby eateries.

The Monthly Financial "Nut"

Sid Carter, who was in charge of finances, informed the group it was very important for them to reach a $1.2 million yearly revenue level as quickly as possible, hopefully within the first 24 months. This would assure the partners of financial "break even," the point where they would be able to meet their expenses and pay down their bank debt. Operating levels above that figure would begin to pay off the partners very handsomely. Revenues below that level would cause some financial strain and might require more partnership investment. The objective, then, was to generate at least $20,000 in weekly sales.

Staff

On the management side, the partners decided to hire six supervisory personnel. The positions included a general manager, three shift managers, and two assistant managers. There were 30 staff positions, including five in the kitchen where there was an executive chef, a sous chef, a dessert chef, and two helpers.

Initial Results

Through advertising, word-of-mouth, and passersby walking in, the café had developed an encouraging early following and fairly robust clientele. However, once March turned into April, then May, the student population thinned out considerably, leaving the partners feeling a bit apprehensive about future business.

By November, cash flow had increased but not yet to the point of break even. The partners met in mid-month and it was agreed that each partner would put in another round of investment funding equal to 10% of their original investment to help the restaurant's bookkeeper stay current with the accounts payable invoices. The next partner's meeting was scheduled for December 15. If business did not pick up for the holiday season, it just might be a tough session.

SECTION THREE
International Marketing

Case 3.1
Tesco, plc.[*]

The Supermarket Scene

By mid-1999, the supermarket chain industry in the United Kingdom had become topsy-turvy with tremendous change in the offing:

- The retail grocery business was already extremely competitive in the UK: nearly all retail companies had announced substantial price cuts in the past year to maintain market share.
- Merger-mania had begun among the giants in the industry with companies like Kingfisher threatening to take away the number 1 share position held by Tesco. (See Appendix A for company information.)
- Wal-Mart had just announced an important foray into this competitive fray by acquiring the Asda supermarket chain, the third largest in Britain, at a cost of over $10 billion. This followed acquisitions in Germany of the Wertkauf and Spar Handels chains.
- In the meantime, Tesco was making several substantial investments in Eastern Europe (Hungary, Poland, the Czech Republic, and Slovakia) and had started expansion plans in Asia (Thailand), where high growth opportunities were forecasted for the coming decades. This meant, however, that investment budgets for Tesco in its home base of the UK were much tighter.

This did not bode well, however, in the short term for Tesco because more than 75% of the company's profits were currently being generated in the United Kingdom in 1999. With stretched resources, Tesco management had to develop new innovative concepts to assure constant growth in their home market. What could they do?

One Option

As the Internet became more and more important in the daily lives of the British population, Tesco management considered ways to integrate their supermarket operations with home and office computers. After all, the information superhighway, once the terrain of young males and teenagers, had developed a mainstream audience, with 39% of female regular users over 21. With some ten million people hooked up to the Net in the UK and more signing on each day, Tesco management strove hard to develop possible linkage opportunities. They also recognized that there could be considerable risks.

---

[*] The case is adapted from an earlier version written in 1999 by Georges Hilbert of Sacred Heart University's MBA program in Luxembourg.

The Company

Since its inception by the founder, Jack Cohen, Tesco, plc., based in London, has opened more than 740 convenience stores and supermarkets, mostly in Britain, but also in the Czech Republic, Hungary, Ireland, Poland, Slovakia, and Thailand. It is the number 1 food retailer in both Northern Ireland and England.

History

In 1919 Jack Cohen invested in a grocery stall in London's East End, and in 1924 he introduced his first private-label product, Tesco Tea. The name was the combination of the initials of his tea supplier (T. E. Stockwell) and the first two letters of Cohen's name. By the late 1920s Cohen was operating stores in other areas of London.

In 1932, Cohen founded Tesco Stores Limited. During the remainder of the decade, the company added more than 100 stores, mainly in London. At the invitation of several suppliers, Cohen visited the United States in 1935, studying its self-service supermarkets, and returned to England with a plan of using a similar "pile it high and sell it cheap" format. Tesco opened its first American-style store in 1947 and went public that year as Tesco Stores Holdings. By 1950 the company operated 20 such modern, self-service stores. During the 1950s and 1960s, Tesco grew primarily through acquisitions, including 70 Williamsons stores in 1957, 200 Harrow Stores in 1959, 212 Irwin's outlets in 1960, 97 Charles Phillips stores in 1964, and the Victor Value chain of discount stores in 1968.

In the early 1970s, however, aggressive competition and a recession battered Tesco, and it was quickly losing market share. As a result of a price-slashing initiative in 1977, Tesco dramatically increased its market share within a year. Because inexpensive, value-oriented brands were best-sellers, Tesco began to create and improve its own private-label brands to compete aggressively on price. The company also began to close about 500 unprofitable stores while opening superstores, some with gas stations.

In 1979, the year Jack Cohen died, Tesco entered Ireland by buying Three Guys (abandoning the effort in 1986). In 1983 the company became Tesco, plc. and added the 40 Yorkshire stores of Hillards in 1987.

Looking for new growth opportunities in 1992, Tesco introduced small urban stores called Tesco Metro. The next year it acquired 97 grocery stores in France from Catteau (sold to Promodes in 1997). In 1994 Tesco acquired 57 stores in Scotland and Northern England from William Low and purchased a 51% stake in Global, a 43-store grocery chain in Hungary. That year it also opened Tesco Express, a combination of convenience store and gas station.

In 1995 Tesco acquired 31 stores in Poland from Savia; a year later it added 13 stores from Kmart in the Czech Republic and Slovakia. Tesco returned to Ireland in 1997 by acquiring 109 stores in Northern Ireland and the Republic of Ireland from Associated British Food for about $1 billion. It also launched its financial services division that year. In 1998 Tesco purchased 75% of food retailer Lotus, with 13 stores in Thailand.

1998 Stores	Number
UK	586
Ireland	76
Hungary	41
Poland	32
Slovakia	7
Czech Republic	6
Total	**748**

Table 1. Tesco, plc. International Representation

Tesco Sales

Nearly half of Tesco's stores by 1998 were superstores that offered food and non-food items, including gasoline (Tesco was the UK's largest independent seller of gasoline). The company's private-label products accounted for about 50% of sales, compared to less than 20% in 1978.

Since market maturity made expansion so difficult in the company's home territory, Tesco management decided to attempt to increase sales through new formats: Tesco Metro, Tesco Express, and Tesco Extra Hypermarkets. The company was also expanding into Asia and Eastern Europe and had launched a financial services division that provided banking and branded credit cards, among other services.

Since 1992, Tesco had undergone considerable growth through acquisitions and had seen its market share in the UK rise from 10.4% to 15.2%. (See Figure 1.) This in turn had led to increases in both product turnover and profit. (The changes in the company's financial fortunes are shown in Appendix B.)

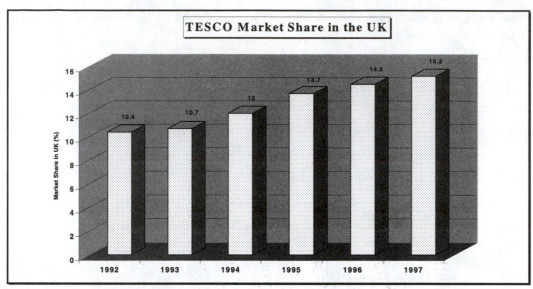

Figure 1. Tesco Market Share in the UK

Financial Data

Operating Margin:

Operating margin in UK	5.9%
Operating margin in Northern Ireland and Republic of Ireland	4.8%
Total group margin	5.5%

Productivity:

Turnover per employee	£146,404
Profit per employee	£8,660
Weekly sales per sq. foot (based on retail area of stores, excluding lobby, restaurant, and non-sales areas)	£21.12

Note: a British pound is worth approximately $1.60 U.S.

Business Strategy

Tesco's main objective was to continually increase value for customers and to earn their lifetime loyalty. Tesco aimed to achieve this through continuous adherence to its core values, which were:

- Earn the respect of the staff.
- Understand customers better than anyone else.
- Be energetic, innovative, and undertake risks in making life better for customers.
- Recognize that Tesco has brilliant people and value their contributions.

- Use these strengths to make customers' shopping enjoyable in a way no competitor can.
- Use intelligence, scale, and technology to deliver unbeatable value to customers.

Ethical Principles

Underlying Tesco's business success was a commitment to upholding certain values and working principles. Tesco, being a part of the society in which it operated, took pains to take care of the interests and concerns of many different groups, including customers, staff, shareholders, suppliers, and people in the local communities close to its stores.

Customers

Customer service was at the heart of the Tesco business philosophy. The base line was quality and value, but customers also looked for a shopping environment that was attractive, well-planned, clean, and enjoyable. New ways of meeting customer needs included introducing customer assistants in shops, establishing a customer service center to deal with customer inquiries, providing facilities for customers with disabilities, and organizing customer question times when Tesco representatives could hear the views of their customers.

Staff

Tesco employed 124,000 people in the UK, Ireland, and continental Europe. It was constantly told by customers that its staff were the company's best asset. This meant the company needed to motivate and train its employees constantly to offer the best possible customer service and to provide opportunities for its staff to develop their abilities to the fullest.

Health and Safety

Tesco customers expected that their food purchases would be safe. The company applied the highest standards in meeting these expectations and made special provisions for those with specific dietary needs. Following government recommendations on the nation's diet, Tesco was the first retailer in the UK to promote healthy eating in its advertising.

Environmental Policies

Tesco was committed to protecting the environment and to using its strong market presence to put its principles into practice. Its environmental polices covered matters such as recycling of packaging, working with suppliers to minimize the use of pesticides, energy conservation, and the siting and design of its stores. Tesco also worked closely with environmental organizations in areas relevant to its business.

Suppliers Relationships

Tesco was working in close partnership with thousands of suppliers in the UK and overseas to ensure products were of the highest quality and delivered in the best possible condition.

The Community

Tesco was very much part of the local communities that it served throughout the UK; employees were encouraged to play a positive role by working in and with a wide variety of community organizations.

The Marketing Environment

The retail market was becoming more and more globalized. All major supermarket chains were beginning to build up an international presence in at least 2–3 continents. Many businesses focused first on Eastern Europe. In a second investment phase, the European food giants wanted to establish themselves in Asia, where big potential profits were anticipated, despite the economic recession in the region. For example, the Belgian Delhaize Le Lion supermarket group purchased the Sunny Supermarket stores in Thailand, which had a huge consumer base of more than 60 million people. Lotus Supercentres were sold to Tesco in mid-1998. The financial invasion by both European and U.S. corporations had begun!

In Eastern European countries (mainly the Czech Republic, Poland, Slovakia, and Hungary), hypermarkets had yet to experience the same boom that had already occurred in the more industrialized countries of the European Union. Many companies invested heavily in these former Communist countries, such as the French chains Cora and Auchan, hoping that as the national economies began to expand under capitalism, the consumer market would grow accordingly.

On the other hand, away from the emerging markets, there was the mature European Union market (EU), where most companies eschewed opening new stores but sought to grow through acquisitions and mergers. For example, Kingfisher, which owned Woolworth and DIY ("Do It Yourself") B&Q, was believed to be close to finalizing another deal in its ambitious plans to become a global player. The company was still pushing through its merger talks with Asda, but it was also in talks to take over a German DIY group, Obi or Hornbach, or Metro, Germany's largest retail group. Besides the U.S. giant Wal-Mart entering the UK, there was also growing speculation that Tesco, Safeway, Sainsbury, and Marks & Spencer were all in merger talks with British and European counterparts.

Tesco's main competitors were other large supermarket chains:

a) In the UK: Sainsbury, Safeway, Asda, Kingfisher, etc.
b) Abroad: Wal-Mart, Metro, Carrefour, Delhaize, Auchan, etc.

See Appendix B for sales and financial data of competitive retail companies.

Tesco, plc. had a total of 60,000 skus (stockkeeping units), of which 25,000 were Tesco-brand products. A superstore sells some 30,000 skus while a small Express store sells about 2,000 skus.

Market Development

Tesco wanted everyone to come in and buy their products, but they primarily wanted to advertise to those shoppers who came to their food stores most frequently. As in the United States, this meant targeting women, aged 21–54 with families of three (two adults + one child).

The Marketing Task

The marketing opportunity was straightforward: how could Tesco develop a strategic marketing plan that could best utilize Tesco's position in the marketplace with electronic commerce to maximize future profitability in the highly competitive UK retail market?

Some of the issues were:

1. Were there enough prospective customers using home or office PCs to make this venture worthwhile? How could this information be accessed? What was known about user demographics that could help Tesco executives decide whether the Internet's user profile matched their shopper's profile?

2. Exactly how would PC owners use a Tesco Web site to their advantage? What should be on the Web site? What information would be most helpful to Tesco customers?

3. If Tesco wished to start a food-purchase service on the Web, what aspects of the service might lead to consumer resistance to use it? These needed to be identified so that Tesco executives could plan on how to overcome such resistance.

4. Would consumers be willing to pay for such a service? How could Tesco find out?

APPENDIX A
Company Information

Location:

Headquarters: Tesco House
                                                       Delamare Rd.
                                                       Cheshunt
                                                       Hertfordshire EN8 9SL
                                                       United Kingdom
Web site: http://www.tesco.co.uk
Phone: +44-1-992-632-222
Fax: +44-1-992-630-794

Officers (1998):

Chairman: John A. Gardiner, age 61
Deputy Chairman: David Reid, age 51
CEO: Terry Leahy, age 42
Director Finance (CFO):   Andrew Higginson, age 40
Secretary: Rowley Ager, age 52
Director Supply Chain and Distribution: Philip Clarke, age 38
Director Commercial and Trading: John Gildersleeve, age 53
Director Human Resources: Lesley James, age 48
Director Marketing: Tim Mason, age 40
Director Retail: Michael Wemms, age 58
Director, Ireland: David Potts, age 41

Stock Market:

Ticker symbol: TSCDY
Exchange: OTC
Fiscal year ends: February 28

Case 3.1 Tesco, plc.

APPENDIX B

Tesco and competition

Sales & income:

		Tesco	Safeway	Sainsbury	Asda	Kingfisher	Metro	Carrefour	Wal-Mart
Sales ($ mil.)	1993	10,807	7,870	13,807	7,262	5,273		20,808	55,484
	1994	12,775	8,322	15,721	7,414	6,750	40,527	25,539	67,345
	1995	15,998	9,428	17,988	8,523	7,720	46,421	29,459	82,494
	1996	18,502	9,268	19,317	9,102	7,993	44,000	29,847	93,627
	1997	21,647	10,790	21,815	11,287	9,317	39,768	28,253	104,859
	1998	26,207	11,672	23,877	12,732	10,460			117,958
Net Income ($ mil.)	1993	563	458	717	246	220		508	1,995
	1994	443	376	211	(260)	347	215	398	2,333
	1995	602	151	849	288	272	594	720	2,681
	1996	713	459	747	344	348	644	602	2,740
	1997	847	482	656	501	445	580	598	3,056
	1998	832	403	802	512	631			3,526
Net Income as % of Sales	1993	5.2	5.8	5.2	3.4	4.2		2.4	3.6
	1994	3.5	4.5	1.3	—	5.1	0.5	1.6	3.5
	1995	3.8	1.6	4.7	3.4	3.5	1.3	2.4	3.2
	1996	3.9	5.0	3.9	3.8	4.4	1.5	2.0	2.9
	1997	3.9	4.5	3.0	4.4	4.8	1.5	2.1	2.9
	1998	3.2	3.5	3.4	4.0	6.0			3.0

Number of employees:

		Tesco	Safeway	Sainsbury	Asda	Kingfisher	Metro	Carrefour	Wal-Mart
Employees	1993	62,374	46,781	120,119	39,207	62,799		81,500	434,000
	1994	62,374	48,503	124,841	37,473	73,067		95,900	528,000
	1995	71,467	47,950	130,000	36,161	43,741	153,209	102,900	622,000
	1996	84,895	47,592	160,435	39,461	77,436	154,291	103,600	675,000
	1997	98,440	49,560	169,631	45,131	77,254	153,800	113,289	728,000
	1998	124,172	50,969	173,775	48,072	83,364			825,000

Financial data 1998:

	Tesco	Safeway	Sainsbury	Asda	Kingfisher	Metro	Carrefour	Wal-Mart
Debt ratio	17.0%		18.4%			22.7%	63.8%	34.3%
Return on equity	13.0%	12.0%	11.8%	13.4%	21.9%	10.9%	12.1%	19.1%
Cash ($ mil.)	48	148	445	31	122	2,729	415	1,447
Current ratio	0.35	0.47	0.71	0.55	1.13		0.72	1.34
Long-term debt ($ mil.)	1,304	1,375	1,523	705	412	3,606	1,457	9,674
P/E high	23		20					27
P/E low	14		11					15
Market value ($ mil.)	18,702		14,093					89,214

Private Label Marketing: An International Marketing Dilemma[*]

Raj Gopal, Vice-President of International Operations, knew Private Label Marketing Company's ("PLM") Executive Committee eagerly awaited his presentation. The 33-year-old company had made a national reputation for itself in the United States and Canada by developing private label products for the supermarket industry. Now, it was time to take the company international beyond North America and invest millions in trying to create the same success in private label products overseas as it had in the United States.

However, in which direction should the company head? West, towards Asia and the teeming Far East, or south, into Central and South America? PLM, a privately held marketing and consulting firm with over 300 employees, did not have the resources to spread its efforts into two continents at the same time. Raj had to pick one. But which?

The Private Label Industry

"Private Label" is a term that connotes the branding of a good or service that carries the wholesaler's or retailer's name, not the manufacturer's. Brands such as Xerox, Pepsi, Tide and H & R Block Tax Service are examples of *national brands*. In contrast, *private label brands* include Albertson's coffee, Shop Rite detergent, Home Depot ladders, and Publix orange juice.

Historical Background

One of the best documented cases of store brand development was that of the Atlantic & Pacific Tea Company, now more commonly known as A&P Food Stores. Since its beginning in 1859, A&P has come to symbolize store brand development efforts in the United States. In the early days, A&P offered its own brand of imported tea blends at great savings to the consumer, who often would pay 50% less for the A&P brand compared to nationally branded teas. When the popularity of coffee grew in the 1880s, A&P imported its own coffee beans and introduced Eight O'Clock Coffee at similar savings. The brand remains one of the leading coffee sellers and is still sold at A&P and other food chains that are members of the A&P "family" such as SuperFresh and Kohl's.

However, broad scale popularity of store branded products did not accelerate until the late 1980s. This was due, in part, to store brands being stocked and shelved by supermarket personnel without much marketing investment put behind them. In contrast, generic products in black and white packages with

---

[*] This case was developed by Prof. Laurence Weinstein and Dr. Sri Beldona. All information in the case is disguised.

just the name of the product category on the container seemed to be more popular with price-sensitive consumers. Store brands appeared poised for failure.

The recession of the late 1980s and early 1990s changed the shape of grocery retailing forever. As profit margins were shrinking for both manufacturers and grocery retailers, competition among supermarkets became even fiercer. Weaker stores closed or were merged with stronger ones. Better locations were physically updated to attract the pickier shopper. Everyone was looking for an edge. Marketing department personnel were instructed to figure out ways to make their supermarket chain different from its competitor down the street. One of the most popular solutions to meet this challenge was the concept that strong store brands could help build a stronger store identity, with greater consumer association and store loyalty to a specific supermarket chain. The race to develop stronger store brands was on!

Today, literally every major supermarket chain offers store brands that are often comparable to leading national brands in both quality and packaging appeal. Store brands now account for 20% of all items sold in the supermarket.[1] In 1998, store brands accounted for over $43 billion in sales.[2] As is evident from Figure 1, store brand sales have been on a steady increase since 1994, and this trend is likely to continue as consumers become more aware of the benefits store brands add to their shopping basket.

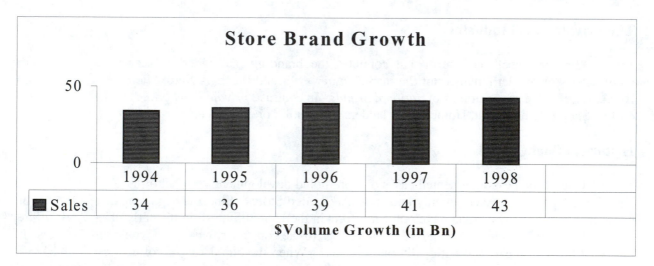

Store Brand Growth

	1994	1995	1996	1997	1998	
Sales	34	36	39	41	43	

$Volume Growth (in Bn)

Figure 1. Growth in Store Brand Products

In a recent Gallop study quoted by the Private Label Manufacturers Association, "75% of consumers interviewed defined store brands as 'brands' and ascribed to them the same degree of positive product qualities and characteristics—such as guarantee of satisfaction, packaging, value, taste, and performance—that they attribute to national brands."[3] Moreover, according to Gallop, "more than 90% of all consumers polled were familiar with store brands. And 83% said that they purchase these products on a regular basis."[4]

Further, the need to offer quality store brands as a growth strategy was being increasingly accepted by top grocery chain executives. In a survey conducted by *Progressive Grocer*, an industry magazine, top executives were asked, "How likely is your company to do each of the following?" The need to stress private label (store brands) received the highest points of any other question in the survey. And the trend towards increasing private label products instore was increasing each year (see Table 1).[5]

Year	Chain Executives	Indep. Store Executives	Wholesalers
1997*	76.9	69.2	86.3
1996	73.1	62.3	85.0
1995	75.7	64.0	84.2

Rating scale: Unlikely (0)   Likely (50)   Very Likely (100)

* latest year available

Table 1. Responses to "How Likely Is Your Company To Do Each of the Following?"

Rationale for Private Labeling

Why do private label brands exist at all? There are several principle reasons. First, wholesale and retail operations make a greater margin selling items under their own brand name than they do selling the same item under the national brand manufacturer's name.

The reason for this is straightforward. National brand prices are fairly easy for the consumer to compare from store to store. Consumer price sensitivity to the pricing of staple items like dairy foods, bread, fruits, vegetables, cereals, and drinks is a marketing fact of life.

Therefore, store mark-ups and margins on such goods are lean. Sometimes supermarkets decide to "keystone" certain popular items and use them as "loss leaders" to pull customers in the door away from competition. If the store cannot make much money on the popular national brands, where can they make the profit to survive?

The answer, in part, is through the sale of private label brands. When a supermarket operation sources its own milk, juice, frozen vegetables, carbonated beverages, and paper products, they can purchase these goods at steep discounts from the regional and national manufacturers who are willing to make the goods and put the label of the wholesaler or retailer on the container.

Why at a discount? For three reasons. One, the manufacturer no longer has to bear the promotion costs for the private label brands. The entrepreneurial risk for selling the brand now becomes the sole responsibility of the wholesaler or retailer. Eliminating advertising and sales promotion expenses can be as much as 25% or more of a manufacturer's costs. Take those away and the manufacturer can choose to pass on those savings to the private labeler in the form of lower product prices.

Two, a manufacturer's plant may be operating at less than full capacity. Rather than face employee layoffs, slowed manufacturing assembly lines, or other types of inefficiencies in the factory, the manufacturer can fill out runs by adding on private label orders. These orders are filled at special pricing levels depending upon order quantity and the leverage that the private label retailer may have with the manufacturer.

Three, a manufacturer willing to enter into private label production could see these sales as augmenting their own brands, thus bringing in "plus" business—revenue they would not have generated otherwise if they had not approached the wholesaler or retailer in the first place.

A second rationale is that retail operations may consider private label as a way to add prestige to their business. Having quality goods under the store's name helps burnish the image of the retailer. Consider J.C. Penney's decision to market their "Stafford" line of clothing. It presents an upscale image for Penney's to help counteract what customers might otherwise think of as buying business suits and accessories from a retailer that used to have a downscale, discount image.

A third rationale is that selling private label brands for less offers the retailer an opportunity to position its operation as a value-oriented or customer-oriented store by saving the shopper money while guaranteeing the product's quality. Would the consumer rather pay $7.79, let's say, for Ultra Tide or pay just $4.99 for Stop & Shop's version of the liquid detergent? Some consumers will still want the national brand name; others, however, with greater price sensitivity or indifference towards brand names may be convinced to buy the store brand if they believe the quality between the national and store brand is not substantially different to offset the savings they will experience if they switch to Stop & Shop's brand.

The consumers in this example believes they have "won" since they have saved themselves $2.80 for the same size container of detergent. Stop & Shop management is pleased no doubt because they have made more margin on selling their brand of detergent than they would have if the consumers had chosen Procter & Gamble's Ultra Tide. Everyone "wins," except for P&G (unless they were the ones who made the Stop & Shop branded detergent!).

Where PLM Comes In

PLM helps wholesalers and retailers to identify opportunities for store brand (private label) growth by category in order to increase/improve the client's overall profit, profit margins, prestige, or value image or all of the above.

As a consulting and marketing group, PLM offers the following core competencies. They:

1. Conduct consumer market research to help guide decisions on which products to select for private labeling.

2. Provide statistical analysis of market trends to determine the success or progress of private label brands in the marketplace.

3. Do the leg work needed to find the right manufacturer to produce the private label product at the right price.

4. Offer quality assurance testing to inform the wholesaler or retailer that what they are buying meets their quality standards and will not affect their consumers adversely.

5. Design the label for the store brand and manage the label inventory.

6. Conduct a "gap analysis" to provide data on what future product categories might be ripe for private labeling.

7. Aid in promoting the store brands by developing advertising campaigns such as "Dare to Compare," which stimulate consumer awareness and interest in looking and considering the purchase of store brands.

Clients

PLM's client list included Associated Wholesale Grocers, BJ's Wholesale Club, Shop-Rite Supermarkets, and the Ahold conglomerate of supermarkets with six different chains, two of which were Stop & Shop and Pathmark. Since its inception, PLM had developed store brands in over 150 different product categories representing roughly 5,000 skus (stockkeeping units).

Competition

Two other national firms competed with PLM for private label marketing and consulting business in the United States. Store Makers, with about 20 years in the industry, had about the same level of business as did PLM. Brand First, with 15 years of corporate presence, was the second close competitor, but Brand First was considered a more distant, third-in-the-running organization. Clearly, the race to grow their businesses at the expense of the other was being waged between PLM and Store Makers.

However, PLM had an important edge over the other two companies. This competitive advantage was their copyrighted business model, which helped clients determine the size of the marketplace and the share their private label product could expect to garner when introduced.

Business Modeling

PLM distinguished itself from traditional food brokers who were typically reactive, rather than proactive, to industry trends. PLM took this strategic initiative because management was committed to a fully integrated marketing approach to store brand execution. Combining a carefully researched understanding of specific consumer needs relating to each individual product category with an integrated brand and retailer strategic plan, PLM's business model (see Figure 2) ensured the product being introduced had appropriate quality control standards, appealing package design and colors, successful sell-through merchandising tactics, and efficient information systems to deliver the right amount of product to the right store location.

Further, PLM also constantly evaluated consumer reactions to their products through both ongoing primary and secondary research. This helped the company make appropriate adjustments in the marketing mix for each store brand to help ensure continuing high consumer satisfaction. This style of professional marketing brand management assisted progressive retailers in their unending efforts to build consumer confidence in store brands and to help make the store a "destination" point.

The Decision to Expand Beyond North America

The domestic market for private label brand consumption appeared to Raj by the end of the 1990s to have reached the mature stage of the product life cycle in the United States. Future sales gains were estimated to be in the 1.0 to 1.5% range in units, so PLM management began to shift gears and started to look beyond the U.S. and Canadian markets for profitable business opportunities. The strategic vision of the company changed from a largely domestic role of helping manufacturers, wholesalers, and retailers develop store brands to a global outlook and worldwide competition.

As Raj considered likely targets of opportunity, he decided not to consider Europe. The European Union countries had a long history of private labeling themselves and store brands already accounted for 40% market share in many consumable categories. However, outside of Europe, the rest of the world for the most part could be considered in the launch or pre-launch stages for private label products. This represented a tremendous business potential for PLM, but also real challenges as to how to allocate their scarce financial, marketing, and human resources in this effort.

Analysis of the Asian Market

The Asian market presented the biggest opportunities in terms of the sheer size of the population in that part of the world. With an aggregate of over 2.5 billion people, Asia clearly represented a marketing manager's dream come true if only PLM could penetrate this area effectively.

However, the supermarket industry in general in Asia was characterized by a large number of independent farmers' markets, small stores and open-air stalls, and, in contrast to the United States, only a very few large, supermarket-sized stores like Wal-Mart or IGA.

Even though the proliferation of television sets and satellite dishes was slowly changing the Asian culture to the "one world" concept envisioned by marketers like Coca-Cola, Confucianism still dominated management and business practices in most Asian countries. Businesses were run like extended families and harmony along with paternalism were the most important aspects of how organizations were managed. Human relationships were considered very important, and individual and group loyalties to the company—and the company to its employees—were still commonplace. The individual was expected to rely on the company to make both business and personal decisions for the greater good of the group. Further, older members of the organization were also accorded great respect; typically Asian business people felt more comfortable and more at ease during meetings when headed by an elderly person. This signified to them someone with great experience and wisdom.

Raj initiated a series of focus groups in China, Indonesia, Malaysia, Thailand, and Singapore to better understand consumer behavior and attitudes towards private label store branding. The highlights of his findings were:

1. Asian consumers have strong brand loyalties.

2. The majority of shoppers walk or use bicycles to visit their local corner grocery stores.

3. Consumers believe national brands signify higher quality, and they often are willing to pay premium prices for these brands.

4. Consumer awareness is critical for successful product introductions and initial trial.

5. Product packaging is especially important in driving consumer perception of what they believe is the product's quality.

6. Cash is the main form of payment.

7. It is very hard for foreign business people to gain the trust of local merchants.

8. Purchasing agents for the few large supermarket chains have enormous influence as to what products and brands are carried by the store. They are truly the "gatekeepers" of the aisles.

9. Unlike the United States, exclusive manufacturers who do nothing but manufacture private label goods simply do not exist anywhere.

10. Local food industry personnel do not appear to have much experience, if any, with store brand techniques.

Asian economies have been racked by currency devaluation in the past (1997–99) and Japan, in particular, has been in a seven year economic slump. However, recent signs suggest Asian economies will become resurgent again in 2000 if the Chinese can avoid devaluating their currency, the yuan.

Analysis of the Latin American Market

Compared to the Asian market, the South American marketplace is relatively more sophisticated since store brand private labeling had already gained a foothold with approximately a 3–4% market share. The benefits of developing and selling their own store brand merchandise was just being realized by grocery store management, but at least it was past "ground zero" when compared to Asia. Progressive retailers such as Santa Isabel, Bomprecos, Disco, Carrefour, Coto, Norte, Tia, Jumbo, and the recent entry of Wal-Mart were all behind the spurt in interest in private labeling.

Business customs dictated a more formal business environment compared to the United States with more importance attached to appearance, business dress, and demeanor. Trust was essential when conducting business and trust was only built over time through social, not business, activities. Networking and insider contacts were probably the most important means of opening up new customers and markets.

Raj conducted focus groups in key South American markets including Brazil, Argentina, and Venezuela. The findings indicated the following:

1. Brokers and middlemen are the key to getting retailers to introduce new items and brands.

2. Distribution systems are almost identical to those in the United States.

3. Excellent manufacturing facilities are already in place for store brand production; some manufacturers have been making store brand products for years.

4. Consumers do not have store loyalties for the most part; they shop where "loss leaders" have been advertised.

5. Consumers spend a considerable amount of time comparative shopping for the best values.

6. Shoppers are willing to go out of their immediate neighborhoods, some times for considerable distances, to frequent larger stores in order to obtain better prices.

7. Buyers are less brand loyal; lower pricing and the perception of similar quality in newer brands vs. more expensive established brands are sufficient to induce them to switch.

8. Visual displays are very important in encouraging new product trial.

9. Consumers have had some exposure to store brands and are just now forming positive opinions about them.

10. It is difficult to find local store personnel with private label experience.

South American countries were considered by Raj to have fairly stable governments and financial institutions. Columbia appeared to be the only nation in grave danger of falling into economic and political chaos in 1999. On the brighter side, old enemies like Brazil and Argentina were signing more cross-border agreements and Ecuador and Peru were mending political fences as well. However, Raj could not foresee a time when the South American market would ever be as lucrative as the Asian market; the population base was just too small compared to Asia.

Raj's Dilemma

As Raj looked at the demographic data and focus group highlights, he pondered over how to translate PLM's success in the United States and Canada to international markets in very different stages in their private label product life cycle. How would he be able to convince manufacturers and retailers that PLM could bring extra consumer value through store brands to them? Would they even be willing to deal with this privately held U.S. company, virtually unknown outside of North America?

Assuming Raj could successfully present arguments in favor of foreign companies doing business with PLM, he still had to decide between Asia and South America. Both markets were attractive, but to limit financial risk and not stress internal company resources, he knew he had to pick only one to recommend entry to PLM's executive committee. With more than $5 million in corporate assets to be invested over the next two years and the re-assignment of at least four senior executives to overseas duty, he knew he had an enormous decision ahead of him.

Endnotes

1–4.   Private Label Marketing Web site.

5.   *Progressive Grocer*, 65th Annual Report, April 1998.

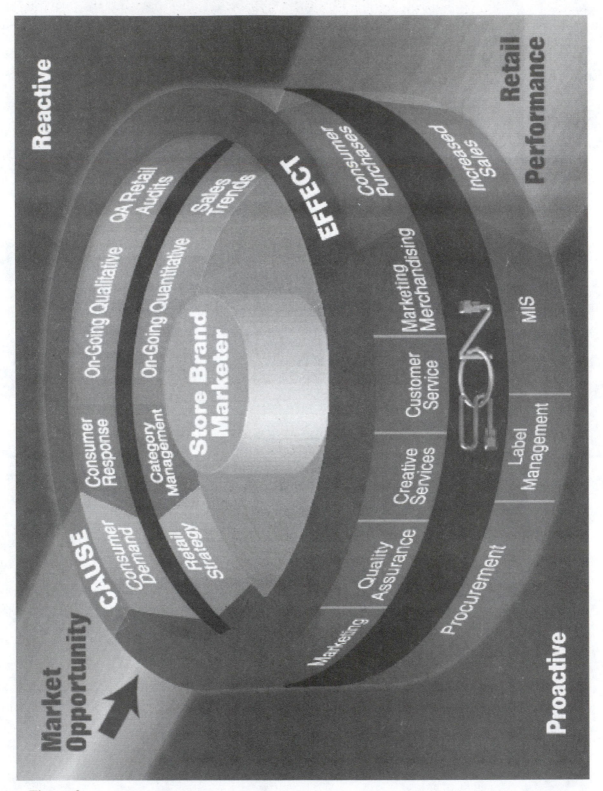

Figure 2.

SECTION FOUR
Marketing Research

One Telephone Call . . .

. . . can sometimes "make or break" your day as a marketing manager. For me, the call from our Southeast Regional Sales Manager, Bob Angler, cast a pall on what had been so far a very successful introduction of our redesigned women's shavers, the Lady Remington models LR 20, 70, and 90, packaged in beautiful, new transparent plastic gift cases. In fact, our package design team, headed up by Ray LeVoire, had entered a national design contest because we were all so proud of the team's effort.

Now the call from Bob. I could not believe what I was hearing. "Pam," he was saying, "You have a problem. I know the women's shaver redesign and packaging looks terrific. Yes, early consumer sales have been strong, but I've come across what I think is a major mistake in the design of the plastic gift case you people developed."

Frankly, I did not want to hear anything negative about the Lady Remington line. It had taken us almost three years from drawing board to market introduction to make the new design and packaging a reality. And now someone was saying we made a mistake? This simply could not be happening!

I First Joined . . .

. . . The Remington Shaver Company, located in Bridgeport, CT, after having worked for a major consumer goods manufacturing company with headquarters in New York, followed by a stint in a midwest advertising agency. Now I was Product Manager on Men's and Women's Electric Shavers, Worldwide for the company that had invented electric shavers in the first place and had introduced them to the public at the New York World's Fair in 1939.

Time, however, had not been kind to Remington. After dominating the marketplace for years, Remington had been overtaken and now overshadowed for the past ten years by Norelco Shavers, a division of the huge Dutch company, Phillips. Besides Norelco, Remington also faced competition in the "dry shaver" segment from Schick Electric, Braun, Sunbeam, and Panasonic.

Electric shavers were used by just 20% of the American population; the large majority of Americans tended to shave "wet" using razors, not shavers. This wet segment has been dominated by the Gillette Razor Company headquartered in Boston. They, too, faced competition, primarily from Bic and Wilkinson, but like Norelco on the dry side, Gillette dominated the wet category. Depilatories and electric personal care products that pulled out hair rather than cut it rounded out the multibillion dollar facial and body hair grooming industry. (See Figure 1.)

---

[*] All names are disguised.

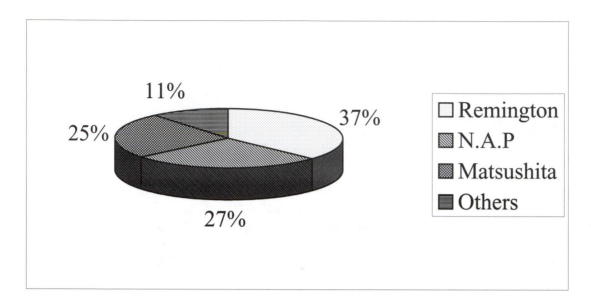

Note: Shares as shown are based on a total of 2,070,000 units shipped in 1995.
Source: Market Share Reporter, Gale Research, 1998.

Figure 1. Women's Shaver Market

The Lady Remington Line . . .

. . . had become one of my pet projects. Sales of women's electric shavers were broken down into two categories: gift and self-purchase. The gift category was especially active around high school and college graduation days, Mother's Day, and the winter holidays of Christmas and Hanukkah. The gift segment accounted for about 55% of annual sales, which made Christmas critical to the profitability of the product line. Self-purchase occurred regularly throughout the year but a bump-up always took place in the April–June quarter as summer approached and women became more conscious of their body hair being seen while they were wearing swim suits at public beaches and pools.

The Lady Remington 90 model was our top-of-the-line shaver. It was a cordless, rechargeable electric that freed women from having to deal with an electric cord connecting the shaver to an electric wall outlet. The retail price varied from Wal-Mart to small, "Mom and Pop" shops, with the average price around $45.00. The two cord models, the economy LR 20, which sold at under $20 and the step-up LR 70, which retailed at $30, rounded out the line.

The traditional packaging for the Lady Remington shaver line started with a colorfully printed, thin cardboard outer container reinforced with corrugated cardboard inside to protect the plastic gift case inside. The outer container sported the large "Lady Remington" brand name and a six-color photograph of the shaver placed in its "jewelry red" nest. Copy included the benefits of owning a product that helped the user avoid the inevitable nicks and cuts caused by sharp razors. The gift case itself was made of a hard, gray, opaque plastic material that made for good protection during shipment to the retail store and, if kept by the consumer, a dependable travel case for business or pleasure trips.

The problem, as I saw it, was the decidedly unfeminine look of the gift case. Yes, I recognized the case had the advantage of protecting the shaver during transit, but its design seemed more like an after thought, or perhaps just a left-brained linear extension of the gift case design used for the men's shaver line. If a hard, opaque plastic case worked for men, the reasoning probably went, it should work for women as well.

The Initial Meeting . . .

. . . with the Design Group caught them by surprise. They had not anticipated my interest in dramatically changing the look and nature of the women's shaver packaging, but everyone supported the concept. The problems were these: Would management support the change? Which materials should be considered? What were the costs? What consumer research was indicated to give us feedback about the new design?

Even more critical to me at that meeting was a consideration of the time frame required for redesigning and improving the gift case. The competitive pressures among women's wet and dry segments were becoming particularly intense. I reported to the vice-president of marketing that our profit margins on the Lady Remington line were deteriorating as production costs continued to increase. Due to low inflation at the retail level, we did not have much "wiggle" room to increase our prices to the wholesaler.

The only other choice was to cut our cost of manufacture, an objective we always considered in theory, but putting theory into practice was very difficult. It was during one of my rare reflective moments during an usually quiet moment in the work day that I had an inspiration. It occurred to me while I was reviewing my product line's Profit & Loss spreadsheet. Could we actually change the women's shaver line packaging and save money too? That would be a double win!

"You're Kidding Me,". . .

. . . Ray LeVoire was saying. "You want to upscale the women's line by redesigning the shavers, creating new packaging, and also saving on production costs? How about we concentrate on one objective, take care of that, then work on the others?"

"No," I responded. "We have to do all three at the same time. That's the mandate I'm giving you. Update the shavers and make the gift case something a woman would want to receive and keep while cutting our cost of direct materials."

Although Ray looked at me like I had lost my mind, I was determined to accomplish these objectives. To my astonishment and gratitude, Ray's design team did just that. Within 60 days of our first meeting, the team presented their recommendation: A clear, thin, feminine (but durable), transparent all-plastic, rose-colored gift case unlike anything ever before used in the shaver industry. It was, for Remington, a decided innovation. The update on our shaver design was more conservative, yet this too seemed successful.

We agreed not to develop a back-up position, but to go to top management with the new shaver and packaging designs and roll the dice. First, however, I knew we needed cost estimates. If we were to go to management and get their buy-on without knowing how much the new package concept and modified shavers would cost us would be suicidal. Nothing upset our president more than marketing managers who did not do their homework in advance of meetings with him.

Cost estimates for new plastic tooling, amortization, and direct labor and materials took another 70 days to procure. It was a frustratingly slow time for all of us, but we were committed to dot our "i's" and cross the "t's" before ever setting foot in the president's office. Finally, Purchasing e-mailed the cost data: Assuming sales in the 200,000 unit range per year over at least ten years, with tooling amortization and normal depreciation, the new Lady Remington package design and shaver redesign would indeed save us money over what we were currently using.

What a victory! We prepared our best "dog and pony" show for the president and gave it everything we had. After more than an hour of presenting our new designs and comparing it to everything we could get our hands on that was currently available in the marketplace, we rested our case and looked imploringly at the CEO. He asked good, perceptive, and level-headed questions about sales projections, upfront tooling costs, the payback period, and projected profitability. We answered them all with aplomb. I was not the only one who put her/his credibility and job on the line that morning. However, as the force behind this recommendation, it was clear to me that any failure along the way with this project would be placed squarely on my shoulders. After two hours of discussion, the president gave us what we wanted—approval to proceed.

Looking back on it, that period of time from first concept to meeting with our CEO was the easiest part of the project and had taken "only" six months or so. Now we faced consumer research testing; development of engineering specifications; and input from purchasing, manufacturing, legal, engineering, sales force, and information technology. Everyone who had a "need to know" was invited to meetings I called to hash out all the details of the new package development project and shaver redesign. At this point, I also asked the advertising agency to offer their input.

To make a long, long story much shorter, it took nearly two years to get the new gift cases into production and ready to launch. We never did experience any potentially project-killing crises along the way, but the workload did fray nerves and managed to place several workplace friendships in jeopardy. I wanted to work "full speed ahead." However, lack of sufficient design, engineering, purchasing, and manufacturing staff required a much slower pace than I was accustomed to or wanted.

The market research piece was actually fairly straightforward and took only three months to complete. Remington contracted for several focus groups among women 25–49 in three metro areas: Boston, Atlanta, and Denver. The appeal of the new case design using mock-ups and drawings was clear and the participants' reactions were pretty much all very positive. To my relief, there were no surprises and no serious negatives.

Finally, we were able to announce the redesigned Lady Remington line at our semi-annual national sales meeting in Chicago with nearly 300 salaried and commissioned sales representatives in attendance. Held in June every year, this was a critical period for the shaver marketing group and the

Lady Remington models.   The salespeople were known to never mince words and often told us confrontationally how we had "short-changed them" by poorly conceived strategic thinking and planning. They were a hypercritical group.

Their reaction? At first there was silence as we used our Power Point presentation to show off the new shaver designs and packaging. Then there was applause and more applause until it became nearly thunderous! We had ourselves a real winner.

The sales meeting was then followed by a presentation of the new shavers and gift cases at the summer housewares show, also in Chicago. Norelco, Schick Electric, Panasonic, and Sunbeam marketing people all browsed our trade booth like we did theirs. Because the men's electric shaver market was much larger and more profitable than the women's segment, the Lady Remington line was not given top billing. However, we were anxious to show wholesale and retail accounts what Remington was capable of doing despite Norelco being the market leader. We gave the "LR" line as much play as we could.

I saw it in their eyes—our competitors were stunned by the beautiful new look of the women's shaver line and the gift cases. More importantly for us, the wholesale and retail buyers who came around the booth were also most impressed. It was going to be a very good summer and fall sell-in period. And Remington was going to be one of the leaders!

You can imagine, then, my horror over Bob Angler's call that day over what he thought was a package design error. His information threatened to take almost three years of careful work and destroy the whole project before it ever really got off the ground.

I Ground my Teeth . . .

. . . while trying to stay calm over the phone. "Okay, Bob, let's have it. Tell me about this big design flaw."

"Okay, Pam, it's like this. You and I can open the gift case no problem. We know how it works and what to do. But our customers do not know the first thing about opening up the case and women are telling the sales clerks they cannot open up the darn things. And because of that, they are returning the Lady Remington shavers and buying Norelco's instead. I tell you, we have a problem and we have to take care of it, pronto!"

"Fine, thanks for calling Bob, " I responded hastily. "Let me look into it." I quickly went around my desk and walked to the display case hung along one wall in my office. I was proud of all of the Remington shavers there on display, including one from the 1939 World's Fair. I slid aside one of the glass windows to the display case and pulled out the new women's gift case placed there just two months before. I held it in my left hand, placed my left thumb on the lower part of the case and pressed slightly in. With my right hand on the upper part of the case, I pushed slightly out and up with my right thumb to overcome the "positive detent" designed by engineering to make sure that when the case was closed it stayed closed. The case opened. Perhaps it seemed a little stiff to my experienced hands, but that was to be expected of all new gift cases. The point was, it opened without a hassle.

Relief Swept Over Me . . .

. . . as I sat back down. This guy is nuts, I thought. Bob Angler is losing it and probably cost me several more gray hairs. Purposely, I waited until the next day to call him back. Perhaps it was spiteful, but I was really annoyed he had made such a bad mistake in judgment.

"Bob, it's Pam," I said. "I've tried out the new cases here and I can't find a problem. They all open just fine. Maybe you just got a few bad cases shipped down there. We'll be glad to replace them."

"So you think. It's not so simple. I think it's systemic and the problem is national, not limited to just the Atlanta area. Why don't you come on down and pay us Georgians a visit? The time out of the office will do you some good and I know you love my wife's cooking. Besides, you need to see this for yourself or else you're not going to believe me."

I hesitated. My workload was crushing and any trip out of the office was usually related to work being done by our advertising agency in New York, or sales meetings, consumer research, store clerk training programs, or new product ideation sessions. Well, this was related to consumer research and it was September so my supervisor could not accuse me of coming up with some hair-brained scheme to have the company pay for some romp in Florida or California, the two favorite destinations for every marketing manager I ever met. What the heck, I thought, I do love Susie Angler's cooking.

Bob picked me up at the greater Atlanta airport and whisked me to several retail accounts where I could see the Remington Shaver line on display. The shavers looked gorgeous and I could not help but feel a surge of pride as we talked to the sales clerks. Every one of them was complimentary and told us they were impressed with the new look. In particular, they said, the gift cases were causing a lot of comment.

Wondering just what the heck I was doing down in Georgia when I could be at the home office, Bob asked if I wouldn't mind eating late that evening. He explained he had set up an opportunity for me to watch first-hand consumers trying to open the gift cases. A retail store manager who was good friends with Bob had agreed to let me pose as a sales clerk and work the electric shaver area as long as I did not actually ring up any sales. I thought this was an excellent idea and went along with it.

The retailer was located in the same shopping center as a Publix supermarket so there was plenty of foot traffic even though it was a midweek evening. I placed several women's LR outer cartons on top of the counter and took the shavers and gift cases out so passersby could plainly see them. Since September was not a big month for electric shaver sales, I turned on my charm and convinced several shoppers to open up the shaver cases and take a look at the newly redesigned Lady Remington line. No obligation to buy and no heavy sales pitch, I promised.

What I Saw . . .

. . . that evening convinced me we had a problem. A serious problem. After watching five women ranging in age from about 30 to 50 struggle to open up the gift cases, I knew Bob Angler had been right all along. Darn it! We had shown the new design concepts to women in focus groups sure enough, but we only had prototypes available then, not actual product. All of us at Remington had been instructed on how to open the shaver cases when we first joined the company. Opening shaver cases was second nature. I never had to think about it. Push in with the left thumb, push up and out with the right. Easy enough if you knew what to do.

I could not wait to get back to Bridgeport. In the meantime, I called from Atlanta and asked manufacturing to stop making any more new women's gift cases. "Put the shavers in inventory," I requested. "We need to make some immediate modifications to the tooling."

On the plane ride home, I tried to structure the issues facing us. We already had hard-to-open cases in the field. Thousands of them. Some were already sold to consumers; most, though, were still in wholesaler and retailer inventory. Then, we had product in transit or in Remington warehouses split between Bridgeport, Connecticut, and San Jose, California. We had cases in inventory in the factory and current tooling that was making new gift cases every day by the hundreds if not thousands. And more orders for the LR line were coming in every day that had to be filled.

Everything would have to be accomplished quietly. To announce or even hint at a product "recall" was out of the question. Our competition would jump on it. It could kill our credibility on the redesigned Lady Remington line and seriously undermine sales of the shavers in their new gift cases for months to come.

I had to think and I had to think fast. Like the saying went, this was a problem you did not learn how to deal with at Harvard Business School, or any other for that matter. I was alone and my career depended on what I did next.

I did some quick figuring on the impact this design flaw would have on our bottom line. My estimates which include new case production, shipping or postage, handling, and repackaging are shown as follows.

Option	Cost Estimates for Replacing the Cases
1. Product already purchased by consumers. Through warranty information, contact consumers by mail and offer to replace the case at no cost by sending them a replacement case with instructions to throw out the old case.	$7.50 each with an upside potential of 25,000 cases.
2. Product on retailer shelves or in wholesaler inventory. Ask for inventory counts, then send replacement cases to each sales branch manager so that s/he can get retail clerks and wholesaler representatives to make the switch.	$2.75 each with an upside potential of 125,000 cases. Payment of up to $50.00 per channel member for their assistance. Potential of an additional $100,000 cost.
3. Product in Remington inventory.	$0.75 per case with an upside potential of 60,000 cases.
4. Product on the assembly line.	$0.25 per case with perhaps a potential for 5,000 cases.
5. Changing the tooling within 72 hours.	$15,000 minimum. Contact the vendor and ask for round-the-clock tool experts to come fix the problem without removing the plastic tooling from the plant if at all possible.

The balance of my sales forecasts for the year showed Lady Remington shipments to wholesalers and direct buying retailers of 300,000 additional units. I needed to calculate the total cost of fixing the design flaw, then amortize that cost across the remaining 300,000 units. If the company president demanded that we recoup these costs by increasing our trade pricing on those 300,000 units, I wondered what that would add to our price assuming we maintained a 70% gross margin.

Case 4.2
West Coast Family Planning[*]

Toby Fisher, director of a local clinic for West Coast Family Planning, Inc. ("WCFP"), a not-for-profit organization with clinics located in California, Oregon, and Washington, was busily preparing for a Board of Directors meeting that was scheduled for one week from today. She was nervous and worried about her presentation.

The Challenge

Her task for the meeting was daunting: whether or not to recommend expansion of the clinics' present family planning services to include offering primary health care. It would be an expensive and risky move, a calculated gamble really, because it meant competing with doctors, hospitals, and existing medical clinics for this large slice of the health care pie. She knew, as well, that the organization could simply choose, instead, to stay "close to the knitting" and its original mission: Providing women (primarily) and men with reproductive health services such as birth control and prenatal care. However, that choice carried risks with it, too.

This truly represented a major strategic decision for WCFP. Toby knew her input would affect the organization for years to come and many millions of revenue dollars would either be gained or lost.

Her recommendations could perhaps save WCFP from its present precarious financial difficulties. Or, gloomily she surmised, sink the WCFP ship and cause the direct loss of hundreds of jobs for administrators, doctors, nurses, nurse practitioners, technicians, clerks, and receptionists who were currently employed by WCFP throughout the west coast. "But, hey," she thought to herself, "No pressure!"

Funding Was Down

Although WCFP was a major provider of family planning services in three west coast states, its programs, funded through a combination of Federal and state dollars, as well as private donations, were stretched tight and each clinic director was told to either increase revenues substantially and/or cut costs drastically. Although supporters of WCFP were typically generous in their giving, the number of organizations aggressively asking for donations had seemingly increased threefold in just the last five years. WCFP had seen its share of the "charity pie" level off with very little real growth after inflation for the past seven years.

---

[*] Names of the people and the name of the organization are disguised.

Toby stopped her work momentarily and rubbed the back of her neck. The tension was clearly getting to her. "I wonder why they never taught you about having to make decisions like this in college or grad school?" she thought to herself. "Maybe if they told us how tough it could be after graduation we'd never want to leave the campus. And maybe I should have taken more business courses along the way instead of mostly liberal arts classes. Well, too late for that now."

Planned Parenthood

West Coast Family Planning was a relatively small player compared to Planned Parenthood, an international organization dedicated to providing family reproductive services on a low- to no-fee basis to any person who walked into one of their clinics and requested services.

The national umbrella group for Planned Parenthood, located in New York City, set overall domestic policy and procedures for the state affiliates as well as raised money from highly structured and sophisticated annual donation campaigns that typically sought to generate millions of dollars from thousands of individual donors. Planned Parenthood operated in all 50 states and had a presence in over 25 countries around the world.

In contrast, WCFP had much more limited resources and was only a regional organization.

Other Issues

Recent violent protests and bombings against clinics that provided reproduction health services and abortions had increased in number, fervor, and sophistication across the country. Religious groups, coming from all sectors of the population, had begun to band together to plan and execute highly visible marketing campaigns to discourage young women, and their male partners, from patronizing such clinics or seeking information about their services. Media hype around clinic violence and the murder of abortion doctors, most recently Dr. Schlepian near Buffalo, New York, had further deterred prospective clients from using WCFP and other providers' services.

Toby considered whether WCFP should start to move its services beyond family reproductive planning. The national mood had become so polarized it was becoming progressively more difficult for an organization like WCFP to focus solely on family planning. Now seemed the right time to pursue more health care revenue by expanding WCFP's array of medical services to include basic health care needs, much as an average doctor's office or hospital outpatient clinic offered.

Managed Health Care

The advent of for-profit (and some not-for-profit) organizations such as Kaiser Permanente, MD Health, Travelers, or PHS taking over financial aspects in order to try to cap skyrocketing medical costs started more than ten years ago. Medical expense inflation had been contained in the latter 1990s, but this dampening effect could erode at any time if labor and commodities inflation recurred. At the same time, managed care had muddied the operating and financial waters for West Coast Family Planning and other health care providers, making it more challenging to deliver consistent quality health care services at low cost.

In response to escalating medical costs in the 1980s that were driving up health care annual expenses with consistent double-digit percentages, health maintenance organizations entered the field with the objective of containing spiraling hospital costs and controlling utilization. If HMOs could cool inflationary pressures ailing the medical delivery arena, they would be hailed as "medical messiahs" and reap the benefits of this success with enormous administrative control over health care delivery and pricing.

Beginning in California, managed health care became the rallying cry across the nation and suddenly individual practitioners and independent, small professional groups found it much more difficult to survive in an increasingly competitive and restrictive environment. The managed care industry itself grew as insurance companies entered this dynamic environment with managed care products. Health care providers no longer had a choice as to whether or not to participate in managed care plans.

For doctors and other health care providers, one effect from being pulled into the managed care system was that they were only reimbursed a certain amount for office visits and the tests, diagnoses, and other services that they performed. In fact, these "capitated" payments were often so low, doctors were forced to try to see more patients in order just to maintain their prior income. Providers who previously refused to accept state medicaid clients because of some states' traditionally low reimbursement rates, were now competing fiercely for these same people. WCFP, welcoming clients from every strata of society, had always accepted medicaid patients, but now found that more "upscale" providers were eating away at WCFP's base of this revenue segment.

WCFP's top administrators had always acknowledged that their organization was a niche player in the health care marketplace. WCFP's positioning was that of a not-for-profit organization that offered no- or low-cost family planning services primarily to young, low income women aged 15–35 who could not afford to pay for these services.

Now, as competitive health care providers were looking to expand their revenue base since managed care had stripped away their traditional high operating margins, it looked as if WCFP could no longer survive on its dwindling number of family planning clients. WCFP's strategic mindset to remain a provider of reproductive health services was being questioned. Challenged, actually. And quite possibly ended forever.

Time for a New Direction?

Toby Fisher, as director of one of the larger clinics within WCFP, was in a management position where she was held responsible for the financial outcomes of her operation. Although all surpluses or deficits were aggregated at the state level, the directors of a major WCFP clinic were charged with supplying estimates of next fiscal year's planned revenues and expenses and whether the clinic would operate in the black or red. Enormous pressures were being applied to the directors to reduce personnel and avoid capital expenditures on the one hand, and to increase revenues on the other.

Toby's clinic had generated the financial results for the past five years, with 2000 estimated (1996–2000). Revenues came from donations, state medicaid, Federal funding, "private pay fees," insurance reimbursements, and sales of prescribed or over-the-counter medications. (See Table 1.)

Year	Revenues	Expenses	Surp./Def.
1996	$925	$950	$(25)
1997	$950	$995	$(45)
1998	$960	$1,030	$(70)
1999	$950	$1,056	$(106)
2000	$965	$1,075	$(110)

Table 1. West Coast Financial Results (in thousands)

Typical expense items for each year's budget include the following. (See Table 2.)

Item	$ Amount
Salaries	$ 393,120
Benefits	71,215
Medicine and supplies	90,720
Rent	75,600
Malpractice insurance	29,400
Yellow Pages	25,705
Consulting professionals	15,000
Utilities	15,150
Building maintenance	16,630
Telephone	12,100
Office supplies	7,560
Lab fees	4,200
Equipment maintenance	2,540
Postage	1,890
Total, direct expenses	$ 760,830
Allocated expenses, central administrator overhead	294,800
Total annual budget	$ 1,055,630

Table 2. Yearly Expenses—Toby Fisher's Clinic (based on 1999 figures)

Patient Visits

Each person who walked into the clinic was carefully logged in and counted. For 1999, Toby Fisher anticipated that over 30,000 patients requiring assistance would come through the clinic. The cost per patient visit therefore was calculated at roughly $35.20. This "rule of thumb" figure was used by organization administrators to evaluate and compare WCFP clinics to one another and to determine the efficiency of their directors.

Asking for Help

With no marketing budget per se other than the Yellow Pages, Toby felt constrained as to what she could do to conduct research into what options her clinic might consider to increase their client base and hence their cash income. Friends with a marketing professor, Dr. Martin Winston, who taught business courses at a regional university, Toby contacted him to help her develop some alternatives. They met at one of the numerous coffee houses around the clinic, which was located near a large state university.

"I know this sounds crazy," Toby was saying to her friend, "but I really have to increase my revenues without being able to use advertising."

Martin responded, "Sounds tough. How do you get awareness now for your clinic and the services you offer? How do new people in the community find out about WCFP?"

"Well, the state organization does some cable TV and radio advertising in both English and Spanish, but the local clinics are solely responsible for making sure area residents and visitors know about the clinic, including the services and location. We rely a lot on word-of-mouth."

Martin pressed, "Do you have any of your own local funds? Any discretion at all over how the advertising money is spent? Is there any money set aside for consumer research?"

"No, no, and no," Toby answered.

"So what options do you have, Toby?" Martin responded.

"We could conduct our own client research. For instance, we could ask our current population what new services they would like to see us offer. That wouldn't cost anything would it, Martin?"

"That depends, Toby, on who designs the actual survey; who you use for your field collection team; who keypunches the data, tabulates the results, figures out if the results are statistically significant; and who then recommends what actions to take."

"Sounds complicated and expensive," Toby answered feeling her energy level going down.

"It doesn't have to be, especially if you can use trained volunteers to do a lot of the grunt work. But you can forget focus groups," Martin added.

"Why? The clients would come in for free if we supplied pizza and soda and coffee, and I was hoping someone like yourself could facilitate for a modest honorarium. Please think about it.

"On another note, what if I recommended that WCFP ditch the niche position we have now and expand our services to include general health care, just like the 'doc in a box' clinics do that are cropping up all around the country? Instead of being a big fish in a very small pond, how about we become a smaller fish, but find ourselves in a very, very big pond?"

"Are you kidding, Toby? You can't do that on your own. You'd have to get top WCFP administrative approval before you moved ahead. It would take months before you could get that kind of backing from WCFP's Board of Directors, if you could at all. You're talking of a radical departure here for the entire organization. And it would come with a hefty price tag!"

Toby was shaking her head vehemently. "WCFP's very survival is at stake. Perhaps they would approve my clinic going ahead with expanding services on an experimental basis to see if other clinics could follow suit. Let's at least start listing the pros and cons of making such a move." Toby took out a sheet of paper. In about 15 minutes, the two of them had made the following list (Table 3), either supporting or negating Toby's concept of expanding services. Although the list was by no means complete, it was a starting point.

Advantages	Disadvantages
Expands mission of providing needed health care to low income areas	Possibly lose focus and niche Increases number of competitors
Opens up many new prospective clients to our services	Requires huge amount of capital start-up and ongoing costs of hiring appropriate personnel
Existing patients could get full range of services	Current image as family planning center may be impossible to overcome
Only way to survive managed care is to have as many members as possible; this could help dramatically	Prospective clients may balk at coming to a "family planning center" for primary care services
Reduces reliance on a narrow set of services	No advertising budget; no existing research; would require prior approval
Could mean difference between surviving or going under	Sizeable risks involved; could hurt image and seriously deplete limited resources

Table 3. Advantages and Disadvantages of Repositioning WCFP

"Well, this has been really beneficial for me," Toby was saying. "What do you think I should do next?"

"Present it to the state Board of Trustees or whomever you have to go to in order to get approval to move ahead. That's my guess."

"And let's say I get the okay to move ahead," Toby continued, "Then what?"

"You're getting ahead of yourself," Martin cautioned. "Slow down. How do you know the Board will approve your idea? How are you going to sell them on something that could require serious up-front capital costs, plus the expense of retraining existing support staff, hiring more physicians to oversee what the staff does, and bringing on board some expert administrators with the competence and expertise to set up contracts with hospitals and private insurance companies?" Martin queried. "You're not even on first base!"

Toby was quiet for some moments, then said, "Let's say you're right, just for argument's sake. So what steps *do* I need to take at this point?"

Case 4.3
Park City Primary Care Center, Inc.

"Our purpose as a primary care facility," Tom Hill, the CEO of Park City Primary Care Center ("PCPCC") was saying, "is to serve residents from the south and west side of the city. We have the equipment, we have the professionals in place, and we have the funding to do the job. The problem is so few people out of roughly 20,000 who live in the surrounding community seem to know about us. It's frustrating. If we don't turn things around, we're going to close, and if we do close, it's going to hit this part of the city hard. Really hard."

Background

The facility currently being used by PCPCC is a 10-story brick building that was formerly known as Park City Hospital. With the advent of managed health care and attempts to decrease the skyrocketing costs of running underutilized medical facilities, Park City Hospital's medical and administrative staff were merged with Bridgeport (Connecticut) Hospital in 1992. Park City Hospital was closed down and area residents were informed they would henceforth have to travel across the city to obtain medical services. Since many of the local residents were low income families, they had to use public transportation, and up to an hour was spent in waiting and transporting time to get to either of the two hospitals.

Local community leaders and action groups in the south and west sections of the city complained about what they perceived as the sudden abandonment by the medical establishment in Bridgeport of their community's health care needs. Political pressure was applied and heavy media attention in the *Connecticut Post* led to intense negotiations. By year-end 1993, PCPCC evolved out of the old Park City Hospital. This was made possible, in part, because PCPCC was granted funding from two area sources: Bridgeport Hospital and St. Vincent's Medical Center, both located within 15 minutes driving time from PCPCC. However, since administrators in both of these facilities were looking to attract more patients to their own hospitals because they too faced budget squeezes, PCPCC was caught in a bind. Neither of the two funding hospitals wanted to lose patients to PCPCC, nor did they want PCPCC to "poach" current Bridgeport Hospital or St. Vincent's patients. Therefore, PCPCC was given very strict guidelines as to how it was to operate; instead of opening all 10 floors of the building, only the first floor was re-opened. And Tom Hill, as CEO of the re-opened facility, was directed not to advertise or in any way promote PCPCC outside of the immediately surrounding south- and west-side residential areas. Given the population density of the area, Tom felt he could make PCPCC a break-even proposition as long as south- and west-side residents became aware of, and began to use, the services provided by the care center.

Community Reaction

When PCPCC opened its doors, the medical staff offered both primary care and emergency services. After an annual review of usage and PCPCC finances, emergency services were dropped in February 1994. As Tom Hill said, "Emergency services turned out to be cost prohibitive. Even though we have just offered primary care since the beginning of 1994, I must say we do a fine job of it. We have some of the best health professionals in the city working here. They're dedicated folks."

Area Demographics

Tom continued, "We experience over 15,000 primary care visits annually for a customer population that is 92% African-American and Latino. The south and west sides have changed both racially and economically. Bridgeport, like many other cities across the nation, has witnessed white, middle-class flight to the surrounding towns of Fairfield, Trumbull, Shelton, and Stratford. It's a real shame, but that's the reality."

Operating Budget

"We have a $1.6 million operating budget funded equally by Bridgeport and St. Vincent's Hospitals. Each facility sends their own representatives to serve on our Board of Trustees. The revenue we generate comes mostly from Medicaid, around 70% of the total, with 23% derived from self-pays and 7% from commercial insurance or Medicare. We have yet financially to break even, however. That remains an important goal."

Services

"We specialize in pediatric and adult AIDS treatment. We served 112 AIDS patients last year (103 were adults and 9 were children) and performed HIV testing on site. Further, over 2,300 children received immunizations last year and we run support on parenting skills. For the adult population, we have had 12 screenings so far in the community on such concerns as diabetes, blood pressure, cholesterol, and nutrition. We provide physical examinations, sick visits, counseling, and on-site testing with our own laboratory and radiology unit. We are truly community-based and provide community services."

Some Limitations

"There are certain services, however, we cannot offer. Our funding sources prohibit us from providing family planning information. Despite that, I feel we can respond to most of the community's other needs. Our building has a total of 126,000 square feet. At this point we are only using 10,000 square feet of that space and all of it on the first floor. We can expand any time we need to. There's plenty of road traffic outside along Park Avenue, an important north-south route through the city. Roosevelt Elementary School is right across the street so we have daily exposure to both large numbers of children and their parents as they enter or leave the school.

"You would think with all the community pressure to keep a health facility open, the subsequent media attention, and such a good facility here that we would be very busy. And at times, we are. However, we are well off from where we thought we would be six years after re-opening. Our funders gave us ten years to show we are a viable primary care entity and could break even or better. But six of those ten years are gone and we are still struggling."

Current Problems

"Part of the problem remains low awareness levels. Each year, the school population at Roosevelt Elementary turns over by half. That probably describes the general population, too. Even if we were to get good 'word-of-mouth' from local residents, half of our satisfied patient pool presumably picks up and leaves before we can develop a stable, solid base of clients.

"So I think there is a surprisingly low level of knowledge about our services here at PCPCC despite our being open Monday–Friday 8:30–5:00 p.m. with late hours until 7 p.m. on Mondays and Wednesdays. By the way, we're closed on weekends.

"I think, too, there are some misperceptions about our care center. People come in all the time and say they didn't know we provided adult services, or adults come in and tell us they didn't know they could bring their children in. It's baffling and frustrating. It could be that we have an image problem as well. When Bridgeport Hospital shut us down after the merger with Park City Hospital, a lot of local folks figured we were gone, never to return. They may still think we're closed. Our front lobby is set well back from the street and prospective clients could be driving by and not even notice people coming in and out."

Competing Centers

"Plus, we do have some competition. There are two other primary care centers now in the area, one specializing in women's health needs, and that could have drawn away some of our customer base. And don't forget our geographical restrictions not to draw clients away from St. Vincent's or Bridgeport Hospitals makes it even tougher to be aggressive and go into the community to stimulate interest in our center. We cannot encourage 'outsiders' to come in to make up our patient shortfall. That would be considered a violation of our funding agreement.

"Finally, we don't have a big advertising budget. We're a money-losing proposition; because of our financial situation we've had to stop new hiring over a year ago and all salaries are capped."

Market Research

When asked if PCPCC had conducted any community-based market research, Tom replied that a study had been conducted in 1997 by undergraduate students in a market research class attending a nearby university. Results were generally positive, with high scores for the doctors and nurses who provided patient care. Negative comments included lack of family planning services, weekend closings, and occasional long waits for services. Tom Hill did not consider wait times to be excessive; these occurred sporadically during the week and were hard to predict. He believed he could do nothing about the restriction placed on PCPCC on providing abortion information or family planning services. Opening on weekends was out of the question given the present budget situation.

Tom's Final Thoughts

"I guess we'll just have to keep plugging away," Tom sighed. "We'll just have to convince area residents we can meet their needs and that we are the best place for them to seek medical care. We still have four years left. There have to be solutions to our problem. We just need to identify them."

Case 4.4
The Race Is on for the Replacement Meal Market

In was mid-year when Steve Kaye received a call from a supermarket client located in upstate New York. The executive sounded upset on the telephone. "Steve," he said, "we need help! We're losing more and more of our customers to places like Boston Market that offer complete, hot dinner meals for families. And it's not just us. It's happening all across the country from the biggest to the smallest supermarket chains. We're hearing it from Publix in the south to Albertson's on the west coast."

Changing Social Morays

The reasons why this trend was occurring seemed clear to some in the supermarket industry: More two-parent families with both working outside the home did not have the time to prepare dinner meals during the week for their families, let alone consider whether they were nutritional or not. These consumers were actively looking for ways to give themselves and their children acceptable ways to juggle hectic life schedules around the need to come up with dinner. Fast-food outlets such as McDonald's, Burger King, Wendy's, or the local pizza parlor had long provided outlets for the consumer's need for convenience and speed. However, some families were becoming more resistant to offering "junk food" to their children on a constant basis because of its well-known high fat and calorie content.

Also, the cultural expectation that the female head of household ("FHOH") would stay at home to take care of the children, manage the house, and cook and bake during the day in preparation for the family's return at dinner time was long gone. Emphasis in the 1990s was being placed on the convenience of food preparation and far less value was accorded to the skills women once needed to have in the kitchen in their role as family nurturer.

Finally, a healthy, expanding national economy with historically low unemployment across the country created fast-rising family incomes. Paying extra to have someone else prepare meals was no longer considered a luxury; rather it was perceived as a necessity and even a reward for hard work and busy lives.

The Implications

The implications of the home meal replacement ("HMR") trend with billions of dollars at stake were enormous for the entire retail food industry, but especially for the supermarkets that had long taken for granted they were the undisputed champions of food sales regardless of time of day or family demographics. Now, however, grocery store executives felt their status as the "destination of choice" for food shopping was becoming vulnerable. Some even expressed fear that the threat from Boston Market and similar operations opening up around the country could permanently and appreciably reduce supermarket revenues.

"Collateral Damage"

To be sure, supermarkets were not alone in studying and analyzing the home meal replacement phenomena. Traditional packaged goods manufacturers such as General Foods, Beatrice, and Procter & Gamble also had a huge stake in this changing tide between the traditional consumer and home food-preparer market and the emerging "new" families where food preparation, at least during the hectic work week was becoming a relic of the past.

Clearly, a revolution was taking place in the retail food market with one industry writer suggesting, "This is not a war between supermarkets and fast food, this is a war between ingredients and meal providers."[1]

High-level marketing executives at national consumer packaged goods manufacturers were wondering aloud what was going to happen to their own product lines if consumers continued the trend away from home meal preparation.   Indeed, one had to wonder if these very same executives felt the time had come to cover their bets and develop their own home meal replacement strategies. This would include, but was not limited to, opening up their own "pick-up-and-go" food outlets that could begin competing with the very successful Boston Market stores.

Store Layouts Don't Help

As presently configured, traditional food retail outlets were poorly positioned to benefit from this burgeoning meal replacement segment. "Addressing the consumer trend toward HMR (home meal replacement) is going to require a complete change in the way marketers go to market and the way retailers position their stores."[2]

So far, supermarkets were losing. Food Marketing Institute research suggested that of the meals prepared by others and eaten at home, 48% were fast food, 25% were from restaurant take-out, and only 12% were purchased from supermarket foodservices. Supermarkets in the United States appeared to configure their product categories as if the "typical" FHOH who food-shopped for her family was:

A thoughtful shopper who had the time to consider 15,000–20,000 brands typically carried by a "super" food store spread over a few thousand square feet. This mom made a lot of her meals "from scratch," valued daily meal preparation, and sat down with her entire family for dinner. She religiously cut coupons and spent hours each week thinking about how to stretch the family dollar.[3]

The more up-to-date understanding of today's consumer behavior was something far different from our nation's view of the 1950s and 60s suburban woman. Indeed, the 21st-century consumer would be "looking for menus of complete meal solutions."[4] Convenience and speed of preparation were paramount. Fresh meals, including fresh-dough pizzas, soups, and even sandwiches, have to be packaged for those buyers who want "easy grab-and-go" dinners they pick up on the way home from work to meet their "latch-key" children.[5]

A few food stores had noticed this trend and were doing something about it. Notably, Trader Joe's, a west coast food retailer expanding rapidly along the east coast, promoted themselves as "a unique grocery store" that offered "high-quality products at value prices" in their 90+ store locations. Many of their food selections were prepared meals; they even offered three specially nutritional meals for children made with organic ingredients under the brand name, "Grandma Millina's Kitchen."[6]

Outside of the northeast region, grocery stores such as Genuardi's Family Markets, Alfalfa's natural food stores, Byerly's, and Wegman's had reformulated their store layouts to reflect more accurately the lifestyle changes that had occurred in our nation's population.[7]

However, some supermarket chain executives remained skeptical they could ever effectively compete in the HMR market. "Many retailers, like Jewel, believe they'll have a hard time convincing people to buy dinner at their store."[8] The problem, they point out, was that "restaurant food has more credibility than supermarkets."[9]

Steve's Response

Charged by the supermarket executive to begin to think about how to approach this very serious challenge to traditional food store hegemony over the dinner food business, Steve drew up a schematic of what the typical food store layout looked like. It is presented in Figure 1.

Steve started playing with different ways the "supermarket of the future" might look to compete more effectively against Boston Market. He knew he had to "think outside the box" on this one if grocery stores were going to have a chance to get back the consumer dinner dollar. He picked up his pencil and began drawing a store schematic. . . .

Endnotes

1. Stephanie Thompson, "Meals With Wheels," *Brandweek*, February 3, 1997, p. 32.
2. *Ibid.*, p. 28.
3. *Ibid.*, p. 30.
4. *Ibid.*, p. 34.
5. *Ibid.*, p. 28.
6. Material available at Trader Joe's, Westport, CT. Store visit conducted Sunday, April 13, 1997.
7. Stephanie Thompson, op. cit., pp. 28, 32.
8. *Ibid.*
9. *Ibid.*

Case 4.4 The Race Is on for the Replacement Meal Market

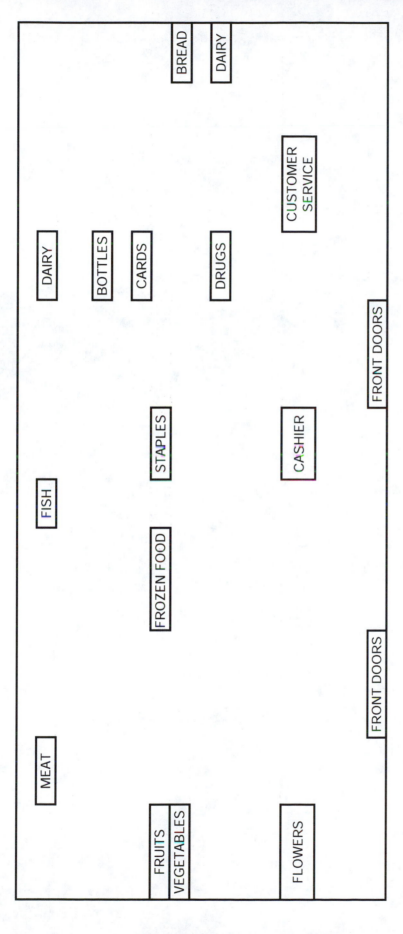

Figure 1. Store Layout

SECTION FIVE
Branding, New Product Development, and Packaging

Background

Tom Nailor loved to snow ski. For the past 20 years, Tom had taken his avid interest in skiing and spent a good deal of his life making this avocation his day job—Tom's been a ski instructor in both Vermont and Connecticut. Downhill had been his passion: bring on the moguls, bring on the trickiest, most difficult slopes; Tom loved to conquer them all.

One day after skiing in Okemo, Vermont, with his wife, Shannon, Tom realized there was one thing he could not conquer on the slopes—his wife's occasional discomfort in carrying her skis on her shoulders when starting or finishing their skiing for the day. Shannon seemed to be complaining frequently about how hard the edges of her skis felt and how they bit into her shoulder blades. The cold weather added to her discomfort; every time she took off her gloves to give her fingers added dexterity in dealing with her skis, Shannon's fingers would just get colder and colder and she felt more frustrated than ever.

To reduce Shannon's discomfort, Tom took the skis from his wife and carried them along with his own. Tom's wife appreciated the offer of support, but Tom knew it was only a short-term solution. Shannon was proud of her own skiing abilities and considered herself independent and very capable. A more permanent solution had to be found. This interchange between Tom and Shannon occurred during the winter of 1992; it was the kernel of an idea that started Tom Nailor unwittingly down the road to new product development and his current entrepreneurial venture.

Making Inquiries

Tom went to several ski shops around the New England region to inquire as to what was available to help skiers with Shannon's complaint over the difficulty in carrying her skis. He found that Shannon was far from alone in having an issue about how to carry her skis more comfortably.

Apparently, a California-based company named "Ski-Tote" had already been scanning the ski industry for new product concepts. Their marketing management personnel understood there was a need to create a product that provided easier portage of people's skis. When Tom saw the Ski-Tote product line, he believed Ski-Tote had at least developed a partial solution to Shannon's problem: By providing a plastic case with a built-in handle to wrap around the middle of the skis, the user could carry his/her skis more conveniently up and down from the slopes.

---

* Names have been disguised.

However, one important problem was not addressed: The Ski-Tote was made for carrying skis horizontally alongside one's body and could not be used if a skier wanted to carry his/her skis diagonally *over* their shoulders. In crowded situations, being forced to carry skis horizontally made for some necessary jockeying between and around people. Near cars, it could also cause some damage by bumping or scraping against the car's body. Ski-Tote was not the entire answer.

Despite Tom's feeling he was compromising on what he wanted to buy, he purchased what the California company called the "Ski-Porter" for $14.95 to have Shannon try it out. The product had a simple hand grip and carrying case with no security lock. Tom noticed he had the option of purchasing the $22.95 "Ski-Tote" step-up model which was larger than the "Ski-Porter" and had a built-in padlock for security. Finally, for $7 more, at $29.95, Tom could have owned the high-end product from "Ski-Tote" which offered a built-in combination lock to the plastic grip handle and carrying case. It was smaller and less bulky than the padlock and a bit easier to use.

Still, Tom reasoned, in severe weather, either the padlock or the combination lock could present real problems to the user who would have to take off his/her gloves to manipulate the security devices to open and then shut the "Ski-Tote." And none of the three models did anything for Shannon's problems of sore shoulder blades. It was a good solution, but not optimal.

The Brainstorm

Shannon started to use her new "Ski-Porter" and she felt the solution was at least partially helpful. It wasn't until the next ski season that Tom made the leap from his wife's "Ski-Porter" product to his new concept, the Ski Hugger® (patent pending). Since he knew Shannon was still unhappy about the way she had to carry her skis, Tom was thinking about how to create something that was more beneficial for his wife.

One day several months later, Tom was working on his son's mountain bike because his son had complained that his seat was really uncomfortable on longer rides. Serendipity struck! As Tom was solving one problem, he thought about how he could dramatically improve Shannon's "Ski-Porter." He would take soft pads such as those used on a bike and add them to the area of the ski carrier where it met the body's shoulders!

The idea worked. With the pads in place around the "Ski-Porter," Shannon's shoulders felt more comfortable even when the pads were only crudely put in place: Tom had simply taken some old bike pads and duct taped them around the ski holder. It seemed to be an ideal product to manufacture for the ski industry market, but Tom did not know the first thing about how to get his concept off the ground.

Tom knew he could not use bike pads for the product if it became commercialized. After considering several options, Tom decided on using the strongest external material he could find and still have a soft product. His decision took some time to coalesce. After a lot of research, Tom chose backpack material and then filled it on the inside with soft padding. The combination appeared to work successfully. Skiers would be able to carry their skis on their shoulders instead of alongside their bodies using ski holders that would feature a soft, but durable material placed around the holder itself.

Thus, the Ski Hugger was invented and Tom's company, Ski-Eze Products International, Inc., was established in Bridgeport, CT in 1995.

The Product

The Ski Hugger was a wrap-around, padded ski carrier with two Velcro straps to keep the skis and hugger in place. The product was made from 1,000 den cordura material supplied by the DuPont chemical company. The cutting, shaping, padding, sewing, and velcro strap addition was accomplished for Tom by a local Connecticut company. Getting funding for his project motivated Tom to find two silent partners; both offered not only money but also advice for the Ski Hugger inventor since one partner was a lawyer and all three were avid skiers.

Cost of Manufacture

Tom believed that with volume production of 2,500 pieces per month, he would be able to achieve a cost per unit of $5.00 delivered from the manufacturer. He and his partners planned on adding $3.00–$5.00 in gross profit to the Ski Hugger so that distributor cost would be in the area of $8.00–$10.00. Due to current diseconomies of scale from low-volume production, the current cost to Tom was $7.25 per unit and his add-on was only $2.70 at most, making for a distributor cost of $9.95. There was no external packaging for the product at this point.

As the first ski season for product sales wound down, Tom had to reduce his distributor price to $8.95 to encourage end-of-season ordering and to help achieve greater retail shelf distribution.

Retail Pricing

Tom had been told by retailers they would only sell the Ski Hugger if they could achieve a 100% markup on the product, generating a 50% gross margin. Special sale periods could temporarily lower their gross margin, but day in and day out pricing had to yield a minimum of 50% at the gross margin line. At the $8.95 distributor price, Tom knew that retailers would be buying the product at close to $10 and would therefore turn around and retail the Ski Hugger from a low of $17.95 on up to $19.95, a price point that represented full margin.

Consumer Reaction

Tom didn't have any consumer research information to inform him whether the buyer's price-value perception would support a $20 retail price level. He could only hope that the benefits consumers perceived they would get from the Ski Hugger were sufficient to motivate thousands of avid skiers like Tom and Shannon to buy his product.

Distribution

To date, the Ski Hugger had achieved only limited distribution in local ski shops around Connecticut and Vermont and also in Aspen, and Steamboat, Colorado. Two of those retailers were Ski Authority and the Darien, Connecticut, Sports Shop. Tom hoped to expand his distribution around the country by hooking up with Ad Specialties, a company that takes over the distribution and marketing of novelty items like Tom's for a 7 to 10% cut of the wholesale price. Although this alliance with Ad Specialties would cut significantly into Tom's profit margin, it might mean a windfall in orders and increased volume levels. If this occurred, the cost of making each Ski Hugger could drop from its present level of $7.25 down to $5.00. He was seriously considering this option although no final decision had been made.

Packaging

Tom Nailor felt the Ski Hugger was a good, basic, product concept and should not be enclosed in a package. Putting the Ski Hugger on the shelf just as it was, according to Tom, gave consumers the opportunity to touch it and check out the toughness and durability of the cordura material while being soft to hand pressure because of the padding. Prospective buyers could also remove the Velcro straps and open up the Ski Hugger to see how it worked.

Promotion

The company did not have the capital to advertise the product. Tom was hoping for positive word-of-mouth among skiers to "sell" the product for him and the keen interest among retailers to talk-up his product with their customers.

Figure 1.

APPENDIX A
Distributor and retailer mark-up and margin computations

Formulas

Mark-up   M. U. %   = $\dfrac{\$\text{ added to your cost}}{\text{your cost}}$

Margin   Margin % = $\dfrac{\$\text{ added to your cost}}{\text{your selling price}}$

APPENDIX B
Tom Nailor's Profit and Loss Statement per Unit—Ski Hugger

	$	%
Gross revenue (distribution cost)	$8.95	100.0%
Cost of goods	7.25	81.0
Gross margin	1.70	19.0
Overhead expenses	.50	5.6
Net operating profit	1.20	13.4
Promotional expenses	0.00	0.0
Profit before taxes	1.20	13.4

The disposable diaper product category, a concept first introduced successfully in the United States by Procter & Gamble in 1968, has reached the maturation stage of its life cycle. Due to stagnant sales volume, market leaders like P&G and Kimberly-Clark have fought fiercely to at least maintain their retail shelf position and number of product facings, if not increase their facings at a competitor's expense.

Product Innovation Was Critical

Product innovation, redesign, repositioning, and "benchmark" cost reductions were everyday "buzzwords" for the marketing managers who had the responsibility of guiding their diaper brands through the marketing battles that raged behind the scenes. Consumers never got to see whose careers were won or lost, how many millions of dollars were spent to keep an established brand afloat, or how profit margins surged or shrunk depending on market results, product procurement, and manufacturing efficiencies.

However, major players like Kimberly-Clark were not the only ones constantly trying to improve their brands to provide consumers with a better benefits-to-cost ratio. Jamie Lee Curtis, accomplished actor in such movies as "A Fish Called Wanda" and an effective television pitch woman for pantyhose, had been credited with inventing an improvement for the common, everyday disposable diaper: She had added a small pouch in front so that the diaper changer could have access to a mini-container of baby powder to apply to the baby's skin before re-diapering the child.

Inspired by Curtis, Wendy Hopkinson, a recent MBA graduate of Sacred Heart University in Fairfield, CT, put on her entrepreneurial hat for one of her marketing courses and had done Ms. Curtis several times better: Wendy had developed a product idea she called "Baby-on-the-Go." (See Figure 1 for her product visual.) The concept was targeted to parents of diaper-age children from birth to four years of age who would appreciate its convenient features and benefits. Ms. Hopkinson described her product this way:

> 'Baby-on-the-Go' is a diaper changing product concept that focuses on the convenience of having all the items needed to change a baby available in one easy-to-carry package. The resealable package will consist of one unisex diaper, one paper changing mat, two small one-use packets of diaper wipes, and packets of baby powder and diaper creme. The entire package will be small enough to fit in a purse or large pocket. (It will) also act as a disposal bag when the diaper change is completed.

Time for a Store Check

Wendy, encouraged by the positive reaction of her course instructor and fellow MBA classmates, wanted to proceed further with her product concept but was not sure just how to move it forward. One of the first actions she felt she should take was to visit a local supermarket and learn more about the category. Wendy drew up a planogram to show the brands, sizes, prices, and number of facings for the major diaper manufacturers. Her disposable diaper planogram looked something like Appendix A.

Packaging

Wendy knew she would have to sit down with a packaging expert and plan on how best to present the product to young mothers. Initially, however, she believed a good approach would be to create an outer cardboard container for the product with a "shadow box" of cut cardboard inside so that the individual items could be snugly placed in preshaped cut-outs. There might be less-expensive approaches, she reasoned, but that would have to be determined later.

Next Steps

Wendy was satisfied that no disposable diaper manufacturer was currently marketing her product concept. The very next step seemed to her to begin talking casually to neighbors around her rural New England neighborhood to see if young mothers, like herself, liked the idea. Wendy approached about a dozen mothers currently using disposable or cloth diapers and they were unanimous: "Baby-on-the-Go" was a hit! She did not ask her neighbors what they would be willing to pay for such an item, at that point, because she believed it was premature to ask until she put together an actual prototype to show around.

Married and busy with a full-time job and mother to a year-old toddler, Wendy knew she could not consider marketing the product on her own. She felt she could, however, conduct some of her own product research and take product development one step at a time. The next thing she did was to cost out the product components using some hunches and the advice of a friend she had who was in corporate procurement.

Product Cost Estimate
"Baby-on-the-Go" Product Concept
(Based on quantities of 10K units)

Item	Est'd Cost of Manufacture
Exterior cardboard packaging + printing	$0.06
Interior cardboard construction, shadow box	0.03
1 unisex disposable diaper	0.08
1 changing mat, paper	0.01
1 packet, talcum powder	0.03
2 baby wipes	0.04
1 packet, creme	0.04
1 consumer literature piece	0.02
Total cost per unit	$0.31

In addition, Wendy knew she had to figure in overhead expenses and promotion costs. That might drive up the per-unit cost to her to about 45 cents. She wanted to mark up the product at least 100% to make a decent profit. Wendy believed wholesalers would look for a mark up of 10% and retailers would mark up the product between 30 and 50%. The final retail price would be a critical determinant in whether consumers would even try the new product, much less decide to adopt it.

Considering the complexity of product development and marketing, Wendy thought carefully about how to form a support network of like-minded entrepreneurs around her or perhaps approach an established manufacturer like Kimberly-Clark to see if they wanted either to buy her concept outright or pay her royalties if they liked the idea and went ahead with marketing it. Kimberly-Clark had the advantage of selling the single most popular brand of disposable diapers in the United States: Huggies. The product's one clear consumer benefit over its competition was its elasticized leg bands that kept moisture inside the diaper instead of accidentally leaking out. Would they be interested in a concept that made transporting a baby and his/her diapers more convenient?

Wendy hoped the Kimberly-Clark Corporation, ever mindful of its rival, Procter & Gamble, was constantly on the look-out for new product ideas and improvements on existing ones. If they were, she might have a chance of getting one of the marketing managers interested in her concept. Realistically, however, Wendy believed this strategy had very little chance of succeeding. Even if Kimberly-Clark management showed some interest in "Baby-on-the-Go," it could take months before any decision was made to proceed and the organization would most likely want to conduct thorough market research on the concept before making any commitments.

The risk also existed that the corporations she approached would drag their feet on making a commitment, eventually turn her down, then possibly move ahead with some type of hybrid version of "Baby-on-the-Go sometime down the road on their own, thus avoiding royalties or buy-out costs. It would be difficult and costly for Wendy to prove her case. Her perception was a lot of companies counted on individual inventors to give up their case against a manufacturer because suing for patent or trademark infringement was expensive and time-consuming.

Wendy believed she had a viable product concept and wanted to continue to move ahead with it. But at this point, her hectic family and work life left little time over for entrepreneurial activity.

Figure 1.

APPENDIX A
Disposable Diaper Product Category

Size **Brands**

8-14 #

Luvs (4)	Huggies (9)	Huggies (Little Swimmers) (6)	Private Label (2)	Pampers (9)	Tendercare (1)	Pampers (2)
□□□□	□□□□□□□□□	□□□□□□	□□	□□□□□□□□□	□	□□

16-28 #

Luvs (4)	Huggies (11)	Private Label (5)	Pampers (12)
□□□□□	□□□□□□□□□□□	□□□□□	□□□□□□□□□□□□

22-37 #

Luvs (6)	Huggies (8)	Tender Touch (1)	Private Label (5)	Pampers (12)
□□□□□□	□□□□□□□□	□	□□□□□	□□□□□□□□□□□□

Over 27 #

Luvs (5)	Huggies (9)	Private Label (4)	Pampers (13)
□□□□□	□□□□□□□□□	□□□□	□□□□□□□□□□□□□

Pricing:

Pampers Premiums:	$35/100 count	Huggies & Pampers:	$15–28/100 count
Private Label:	$15–22/100 count	Huggies Overnights:	$43/100 count

Case 5.3
Stew Leonard's Dairy A:
Does Downsizing the Packaging Make Sense?

A Problem or an Opportunity?

It was the middle of a blustery spring afternoon along Route #1 in Norwalk, Connecticut. This busy local artery in Fairfield County is also referred to as Westport Avenue, but mainly by post office personnel. More commonly, Route #1 is called "The Boston Post Road" by many locals since it has been used in Revolutionary War days as the major land communication and postal link between New York City and Boston and points in between.

I remember the day distinctly because I noticed how the wind was kicking up leftover sand from the town's winter sand spreaders. The tiny grains of sand were swirling in the air like snakes trying to reach the clouds. The sand stung my eyes and face as I walked towards the entrance of the renowned supermarket, Stew Leonard's Dairy.

I had an appointment to see Stew Leonard, Jr., CEO of Stew Leonard's Dairy in response to a call he had made to me a few days earlier. Although I was a few minutes ahead of schedule, Stew, Jr., immediately came out of his office after he was alerted to my presence and asked me to come into his office. "I don't know if I have a problem or an opportunity. However, I *do* know one thing; everyone in the office is up in arms with one another. Unfortunately, it seems battle lines have been drawn with no one backing down."

Background

Stew Leonard's Dairy stores are located in Norwalk and Danbury, Connecticut, with a third location just opened in Yonkers, New York. They are well-known to local area shoppers as well as to consumers who drive to Connecticut regularly from nearby New York, New Jersey, Pennsylvania, Massachusetts, and Rhode Island just to buy their food at the dairy.

Referred to as the "Disney" of retail food operations, management of this three-store chain tries hard to make the food shopping experience unlike that of any other supermarket in the world. A small farm outside the store greets visitors and features goats, hens, roosters, rabbits, and ducks. A garden shop, and during summer months, a covered area where families can buy and eat barbecued meat, fish, and corn are the next places to visit. Inside, fun themes and animated characters with background music delight young and old alike with their corny and sentimental versions of music, which provide a "soft sell" family shopping environment.

Founded by Charles Leo Leonard in 1924, the company has featured its milk bottling operation since moving to its present location in 1969. The first store on the site offered shoppers twelve different dairy items and a drive-through convenience window. The first building had grown and changed dramatically through 21 different additions and renovations.

Stew Leonard's Dairy was listed in the *Guinness Book of World Records* as the store with the fastest moving sales per square foot (about ten times the industry average!), and was featured in *Ripley's* "Believe It or Not." The dairy has been a regular stopping-off point for businesspeople from around the world to study how the Leonards developed their marketing mix strategies, and was cited by Tom Peters in his book, *The Passion for Excellence*, for management commitment to quality.

The Meeting

Stew swung around his desk and sat down with a sigh. "Remember when you and I started discussing the changing demographics in Fairfield County? How information we had poured over suggested there were more single-person household numbers emerging from the data?"

I nodded in agreement. We had studied available census data and then spent a considerable amount of time on the findings from a base-line segmentation market research study I had undertaken for the store several years earlier. It showed the "typical" shopper to be female, age 32, Caucasian, from Norwalk or Stamford, with a family size of 3.2 people. The store from its inception has always catered to the family unit because it was taken for granted that this demographic group was the dominant economic force in the region.

Product package size and volume discount pricing reflected this strategic decision in every department, including diary, meat and fish, farm produce, and even snack items like potato chips, pretzels, and soda. The store always features some item weekly that is keystoned at cost or near cost to motivate shoppers to stop by the dairy.

What the survey did not focus on were the number of individuals who responded to the inperson interview by saying they lived alone. This phenomenon of "live-alone" people had several causes. People in their twenties and thirties were delaying marriage; others were divorced living alone or had never married. Some had out-lived their partners and chose to continue to live independently. All these single-person households had upset the theory of the family life cycle that most Americans moved "herd-like" from being single, to newly married, to having full nests, and then experiencing empty nests.

"I wish we had more hindsight," Stew, Jr., continued, "I wish we had used part of that segmentation study to figure out just how many of our shoppers lived alone and what preferences they have when it comes to package size."

"Stew," I responded, "that wasn't the purpose of the study."

"Yeah, yeah, I know that. But now I wish it had been," Stew rejoined. I could see the tension in his face. "You see, our store has always positioned itself as a great place to get the highest quality food items at reasonable prices. We're totally set up for families. Our package sizes for food, especially dairy and meat, are for the younger families who have a couple of growing kids. That's what the segmentation study confirmed for us."

Losing the Singles Audience

"However, I've just had several meetings with my store managers and several of them think we should shift our strategy. One or two are absolutely convinced we are losing significant business because working singles in the area only come into our store to buy their hot or cold salads at lunch time and then march right out without purchasing anything else. And you know why? They look at our blocks of cheese or large-size yogurt containers and say to themselves, 'No way am I going to buy something this big. It will never be eaten up before it goes bad.' And if they think that way about the prepackaged cheese or the yogurt, they're probably thinking that way about a hundred other products we sell in the store.

"So I'm thinking, sure, it might make sense to downsize our packaging. We shouldn't be losing that business to our competitors like Stop & Shop, Shaw's, Waldbaum's, or Big Y. Then I approach the finance folks and they go absolutely bananas when they hear about what some managers have suggested."

I interrupted, "Why, what's their beef?"

"In a nutshell," Stew countered, "They advise me I'm crazy to trade down. According to their argument, if we reduce the average size of the prepackaged cheese, say from one and a half pounds to three-quarters of a pound, then all the people who are buying the larger package sizes may simply change their buying behavior and purchase the smaller sizes along with the people who shop here who live alone. Yes, the single-household folks will be happy, but the bottom line for us is that we will lose cheese sales because we've encouraged all of our shoppers to buy less. Even the ones who used to buy larger sizes of cheese will now think of themselves as being 'thriftier' since they could try to get along with the smaller sizes."

I offered, "Have you thought of trying to set up a separate section in the store and call it 'The Singles Place' or some such designation?"

"No I haven't," Stew said. "I'm not convinced that would do us any good anyway. What would stop moms with families from buying their produce there anyway? Do we position a cop there and ask," at this point Stew, Jr. lowered his voice and put on an 'attitude' and continued with, "'Hey, lady, you can only buy food from this display if you live alone. Do you? 'Cause if you don't, forget it! You have to buy the larger packages in the rest of the store.'"

Adjusting back to his normal inflection, Stew continued, "You can see how ridiculous the whole notion of a separate area might become. I went over to Purchasing and told them about how we were discussing the whole idea of downsizing the packaging and I asked them for their opinion. It didn't take long for World War III to erupt. It was like they had rehearsed their lines or something. I couldn't believe it. They were truly hostile to the idea.

"That leaves me in the middle and I need to make some decisions. Do I just give up all the business generated by people who live alone or do I reposition the store and go after thousands of shoppers who probably are avoiding the dairy?

"Stew Leonard's is a unique place where all shoppers are able to save money because we carry just 1,000 brands, not 12,000 to 15,000 brands like a typical supermarket. We choose to stock the larger volume sizes of most brands because it saves shoppers money on a per-pound basis. Our competition, besides the supermarkets, includes the Costco's, the Price Clubs, and the Sam's Clubs mushrooming around the tri-state area. Most consumers understand that buying in larger quantity means they can cut their food bills.

"Let's assume we downsize some of the packaging," Stew continued. "If we were to carry smaller sizes of produce we'd be taking up room from the bigger sizes where we make more margin. Our costs would go up since we'd be stocking and inventorying more individual skus, and our margins would shrink. On the other hand, we'd increase our customer numbers and hopefully our total revenue. It's a tough trade-off. I frankly don't know what to do."

The conversation continued for another few minutes, then Stew asked me for some marketing insights. This was going to be an interesting consult.

SECTION SIX
Pricing and Distribution

The Day Was Winding Down

Susan Samet sat gloomily in her folding metal chair. She had spent the entire day in this upscale, New England town waiting for someone, anyone, to come by her booth at the juried artist's fair and buy one of her paintings. ("Juried" means a panel of art experts reviews artists' submissions and selects only those who the experts feel reach a certain level of proficiency. Since many exhibits and/or fairs have only limited space, competition among artists to get into a juried exhibit can be fierce.) Susan had decided to display 12 of her framed and matted watercolors with price tags ranging from $150 to $500. See Appendix A for several examples of her artwork.

This particular Saturday involved seven hours of sitting and waiting patiently, discussing her artwork with kind passersby, hoping all the while she did not seem overly anxious, wondering why other artists were selling their pieces but not her, and watching the summer sky slowly fade into dusk. In the pit of her stomach, Susan had the same gnawing feeling of doubt, of collapsing self-esteem, she had felt on other occasions when her artwork did not sell particularly well. Maybe her vibrant watercolor paintings were just not good enough. Too "pretty," perhaps, or perceived as "cute," or "fanciful," or, heaven forbid, too "amateurish" for the local art patrons to consider her efforts seriously.

She was trying not to feel devastated by the day's events when she became aware of someone looking around her booth area. Susan recognized the person as a fellow artist who had seemed to receive a lot of attention during the day and who probably had sold at least half a dozen pieces of her artwork. The woman spoke up, "I hope you don't mind my coming around your booth area. Your works are really quite good and I'm admiring them."

Susan tried not to sound downcast, but her voice came out feeling tired and a little bitter, "Well, at least someone thinks I might have talent! I haven't sold a thing today and I have to admit that I'm feeling really down about it." Susan introduced herself and found out she was talking to Tara Hudson[*], an artist from New Jersey who painted mainly in oils.

Tara responded with, "I hope you don't mind my offering you a little advice, Susan. You really do have talent and your paintings should be selling. I think you have them priced too low for this area. This town is filled with extraordinarily wealthy people who commute and work in New York City. They expect to pay a handsome fee for the artwork they buy and your pieces are simply priced too low. They may have a feeling that your artwork isn't worth considering because it's priced so inexpensively."

---

[*] Name disguised.

Susan was floored. "You mean, if I *increase* my prices, my artwork will have a better chance of selling?"

"That's right," Tara answered. "You heard me correctly. Knowing your audience's buyer behavior and what motivates them to make an art purchase is critical to success at artist's fairs like this one. You need to figure that out before you put a price tag on any of your artwork."

Susan thought quietly. She had already experienced modest success as an artist and her reputation as a watercolorist was growing steadily. One of her paintings had even been mentioned favorably in *The New York Times*. But here she was getting some good advice for sure, yet feeling like a rookie and wondering why she hadn't known better. However, Susan always felt uncomfortable when pricing her pieces and never really was sure how artists figured that all out any way.

The Next Day

Susan talked about Tara's comments with her husband, Michael, when he returned to their booth area a few minutes after the other artist had left. Michael was supportive of Susan's talent and always accompanied her to the artist's fairs she entered and for which she had to pay a stiff entrance fee for showcasing her artwork.

They discussed what to do. In the end, after some heated conversation about whether to risk Sunday's effort by raising the price of Susan's artwork, they agreed it was worth experimenting. The $150 to $500 price range was shifted to $250 on up to $800. Not an inordinately large increase, but one that Susan felt still carried some amount of risk of buyer resistance.

The next day dawned bright and clear. Nervous, but with great anticipation, Susan opened her booth and waited for customers. She didn't have long to wait. She sold her first painting by 9:30 a.m., and by the time she closed her booth at 4 p.m. that day, four more paintings had been sold. Between cash and personal checks (she did not accept credit card payments), Susan had nearly $2,000 in her pocket!

Personal History

As a child, Susan loved to draw, spending hours with crayons, coloring books, and pads of paper from her father's office. Even though she attended a private high school with a reputation in the arts, Susan never went near the art studio. She started college at Russell Sage, but decided to transfer to Boston University to attend their School of Fine and Applied Arts. However, careless mistakes on her application form got her admitted to the College of Liberal Arts instead. Not wanting to get set back a year in her studies, Susan majored in Art History and never did get the chance to develop her artistic side while in Boston. In 1968, she married Michael Samet and did not return to art for nearly 15 years.

It was many years later, when her two children were in their teens, that Susan decided to try seriously to develop her artistic talent. She took watercolor classes at the Art League of Long Island, New York, and was fortunate to study with several extraordinary teachers, including her very first who was passionate about color. At this point, she recollected, a whole new set of experiences opened up to her.   To her surprise, people expressed an interest in buying her work and she began to exhibit her watercolors in 1992. (See Appendix B for a partial list of the exhibits.)

Figuring Out the Demand Curve

The week following the artist's fair was a busy time for Susan.   Knowing the importance, however, of making some key decisions on her pricing strategy, she took a break from her painting to consider the nagging issue over just how to figure out what prospective buyers would be willing to pay for her work.   Susan took out some graph paper and developed a demand curve, which, after several modifications, is replicated here (see Figure 1).

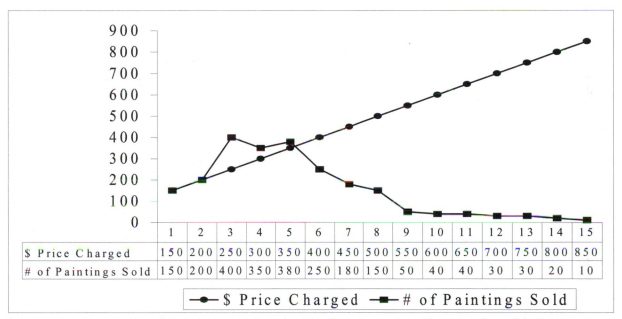

	1	2	3	4	5	6	7	8	9	10	11	12	13	14	15
$ Price Charged	150	200	250	300	350	400	450	500	550	600	650	700	750	800	850
# of Paintings Sold	150	200	400	350	380	250	180	150	50	40	40	30	30	20	10

Note: Figures disguised for confidentiality. To simplify the chart, an average price was taken of original watercolors and prints.

Figure 1. Kinked Demand Curve

Her very first effort at understanding how price affected her sales was based largely on estimates. That was over five years ago. Since then, Susan has sold over 400 paintings and reprints of her originals. From that experience, she now believed she faced a "kinked" demand curve for her artwork.

The Upcoming Art Season

Susan decided to enter six different juried art exhibits for the coming season. The six scheduled exhibits were:

Approximate Dates	Name of Exhibit or Fair
End of April	Sloane-Kettering Cancer Center—Fundraising Exhibit
Second weekend in July	Wickford, Rhode Island, fair
First weekend in August	Westhampton Beach, New York
Last weekend in Sept.	Gracie Square, New York City
First weekend in Oct.	Armonk, New York
Third weekend in Oct.	Newark Museum Fundraiser in Montvale, New Jersey

Susan's objective was to sell at least 100 paintings and reprints a year, but much would depend on her pricing decisions.

Product

Susan liked to work primarily in standard size and format watercolors; occasionally she made prints of her best artwork and sold the prints at roughly one-third the price of the original. Also, Susan was developing her photography skills and recently won a $400 prize at a juried photography exhibit. However, watercolors remained her passion.

Price

When determining how to price her artwork, Susan would nearly double her asking price if her watercolors were being shown in an art gallery. Gallery owners typically charged one-half of the retail sales price as their commission for hanging and showing the artwork. Therefore, Susan had to increase the retail price to cover the gallery's commission over what she would normally ask at fairs. The kinked demand curve shown earlier are art exhibit and fair prices, not gallery prices which run $200 to $500 more.

Individual pieces were priced according to size. Then the price was adjusted depending upon whether Susan felt a particular piece was more or less successful than the "average" piece. A particularly strong watercolor was adjusted upwards; a piece that disappointed Susan in its final composition and/or color choice was lowered and priced to sell fairly quickly to remove it from inventory.

The sizes Susan worked in and the typical price for that size are shown as follows.

Size	Price Range
11 × 11	$ 75 — $ 125
15 × 15	200 — 250
16 × 20	250 — 375
20 × 20	300 — 400
22 × 25	325 — 500
27 × 30	550 — 1,500
33 × 40	900 — 1,800

Place

Besides the six shows in which Susan planned to exhibit her paintings in the coming year, she also hoped to gain exposure through local art galleries on Long Island and in nearby New York City, New Jersey, and Connecticut, if she could. Usually, two to three gallery owners asked Susan to exhibit her work in their retail locations each year and she would end up selling from three to five pieces per gallery this way.

In 1998, Susan felt she got a good break when Grohe/Signature Galleries decided to display her artwork in three of their galleries in Connecticut and Massachusetts, but the higher asking prices necessitated by the retailer's mark up had ended with disappointing sales results. Susan did not submit slides of her work to this gallery for 1999.

Several art guilds had recently approached Susan and asked if she wanted to include her artwork in their Internet Web sites. She had not committed herself as yet, but Susan felt this chance for wider exposure could be very exciting and remunerative.

Promotion

Susan did not invest in any advertising or public relations releases for herself in the local media. She had business cards printed up (see Appendix C) in case prospective buyers wanted further information or her telephone number to keep in touch.

Buyer Behavior

Susan had never taken a college marketing class. In discussing her pricing issues with a friend who taught marketing classes at a nearby university, she was referred to a buyer behavior model used to instruct students on how consumers behaved when making a considered purchase. It was helpful in that it showed how complex the buying decision could be, especially when the value of artwork could be so difficult to gauge.

Decisions Had to Be Made

With the art season opening up shortly, Susan was faced with making important pricing decisions that would help propel—or could possibly stall—her career as a watercolorist. She looked at the demand curve she had created the previous fall. With a sigh, she asked herself: What have I learned from it? At what price would I maximize my sales in terms of number of original watercolors and prints sold? At what point would I maximize my dollar revenue? Which should be my goal?

Did the curve suggest Susan should increase her prices? If so, what would her new price schedule look like? Was she in a price elastic or price inelastic environment?

APPENDIX A
Examples of Artwork

APPENDIX B
Partial List of Exhibits

SUSAN SAMET
109 STOOTHOFF ROAD • EAST NORTHPORT, NY 11731 • (516) 368-4790

SELECTED EXHIBITIONS

1999 • Catherine Lorillard Wolf Art Club, NYC
- Heckscher Museum (award)
- Shelter Rock Gallery, Manhasset, NY * reviewed by Newsday

1998 • Heckscher Museum (award)
- *Dan's Papers* cover painting
- Firehouse Gallery, Nassau Community College
- Smithtown Arts Council Photography Exhibit
- New York Institute of Technology, Solo Exhibit
- Signature Galleries, Westport, CT; Mashpee, MA
- Newark, NJ Museum Benefit Exhibit
- Vincent Louis Gallery, NYC

1997 • Firehouse Gallery, Nassau Community College (award), * reviewed by NY Times
- Chelsea Center, Muttontown

1996 • Art League of Long Island, Solo Exhibit
- New York Institute of Technology
- Hechscher Museum (award)
- Newark NJ Museum Benefit Exhibit

1995 • Allied Artists of America
- Visual Arts Alliance of Long Island
- Jericho Library (solo exhibit)
- Suburban Art League (award)

1994 • National League of American Pen Women
- Art League of Nassau County

1993 • National League of American Pen Women
- Art League of Nassau County

1992 • Catherine Lorillard Wolfe Art Club, NYC
- Community Gallery, Northport (solo exhibit)
- Graphic Eye Gallery, Port Washington
- Huntington Township Art League (award)

EDUCATION
Studied with Paul Wood, Stan Brodsky, Carl Molno, Sal Tortora,

AFFILIATIONS
- National Association of Women Artists
- Art League of Long Island

COLLECTIONS
Memorial Sloan Kettering Cancer Center

APPENDIX C
Business Cards

SUSAN SAMET
WATERCOLORS
516-368-4790

Susan Samet is an artist who loves color. She turns the ordinary extraordinary with her bold use of vibrant colors. Her work can be found in corporate and private collections.

Case 6.2
The Devaney Paper Company: A Distribution Dilemma[*]

The four Devaney brothers had never faced such sharply divided opinions among themselves since taking over the business from their parents. Just what were they going to do?

Reminiscing

Tom Devaney, past president of the Devaney Paper Company, now recently retired, was reminiscing about the organization his father had started during World War II. "You know," he said, "when I think back to how hard we had to work to survive, I'm amazed that we did. So many other paper companies went out of business, but our Mom and Dad, Elizabeth and George Devaney, bested them all. And their four sons, me included, picked up what they left us and made it even better. I'm proud of that."

How It All Started

George Devaney faced a tough choice during World War II. He was a chemical engineer by trade and education working on matching colors for a paper printing company, but he found the work unchallenging and tiresome. He felt he had two choices if he left his job: re-enlist into the Navy as a Chief Petty Officer and try to feed a large family on military pay or take a huge leap of faith and become an entrepreneur.

After discussing the pros and cons with his wife, Elizabeth, the two decided on a course of action that would lead, nearly 60 years later, to a powerhouse of a company with revenues of more than $100 million annually.

Building on Strength

George knew a lot about the paper industry and how to print quality work from his previous employment. His first decision was to purchase a gravure press in Rhode Island for less than $100 that seemed little more than scrap metal. Within 30 days, George got the press up and running and he was in business.

George moved his family to the middle of Massachusetts and rented some unused space from an established New England paper company. The budding entrepreneur put out feelers in the paper industry for people who wanted to take advantage of his expertise in using Argentine Silver Print, a special and very complicated process of making high-quality silver foil. George made a sample book for potential clients to see his capabilities as a printer and, in turn, received immediate interest.

---

[*] All names are disguised.

His next move was to find a press that would print on wood grain. This gave George an opening into surrounding manufacturing plants that shipped goods via wood boxes that required their company identification on the outside. Several years later, having established himself as a reputable and very reliable one-color printer, George purchased a third press for $2,000 in 1951. The press owner at the time considered the two-color gravure press just a "pile of junk" on two pallets in a back storeroom. For George, it was an important move forward because he now had the technical ability to branch out into work that required more than one color.

Opportunity Kept Knocking

Exhibiting the talent that suffuses other successful entrepreneurs, George was always keeping an eye out for other presses to buy at rock bottom prices as competitors fell by the wayside. He saved thousands of dollars of capital costs through his technical and engineering wizardry. In 1954, George purchased a two-color press from a nearby company that he would eventually be able to adapt to run three-color jobs. In 1964, the Southwest Paper Company "virtually gave away" two wide presses and a winding machine to the Devaneys. In the early 1970s, George purchased a four-color press from a mid-Atlantic concern going bankrupt. The company obtained another four-color press and two Flexo presses in 1988 from a competitor closing its doors in upstate New York.

By this time, four sons had joined the business and George and Elizabeth had retired. Yet, the family's business expansion strategy remained exactly the same: strike quickly and move smartly when used presses became available at fire sale prices that could help the Devaneys move into new market territory.

In 1992, a five-color gravure press was sold to the Devaneys by a midwestern firm. In 1995, a six-color Flexo press was obtained from a Texas firm going belly-up. That same year, an eight-color press was purchased by a company desperate to get it off its main production floor. The press's original cost new was at least $2.5 million. The Devaneys paid $75,000 for it plus $350,000 for transportation and installation!

The Distribution Network

Today, even though the Devaney Paper Company, still headquartered in central Massachusetts, is one of the largest converters in the world of high-quality paper products such as gift wrapping, silk and silver foil printing, and paper embossing, the consuming public has probably never heard of this multi-million dollar operation. That's because George Devaney decided from the beginning not to have a direct selling relationship to retailers. Instead, he chose to sell to distributors and created a two-step distribution process for his paper products.

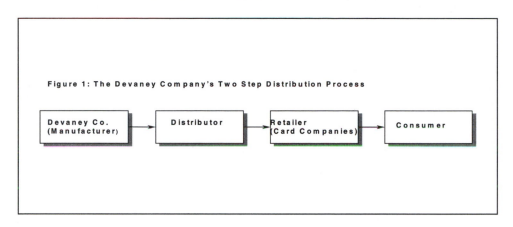

Figure 1: The Devaney Company's Two Step Distribution Process

Devaney Co. (Manufacturer) → Distributor → Retailer (Card Companies) → Consumer

Over the years, George Devaney's initial decision had created a firm commitment from the company to remain loyal to Devaney's distributors. Why? Because it was through these distributors that Devaney had been able to reach, and sell to, such top-quality customers as Neiman-Marcus, Lord & Taylor, and Macy's—to name just a few of their retail clients.

However, this commitment to sell only through distributors, and never directly to the end user or retailer, was tested dramatically several years ago when an international greeting card company, Stillwater Incorporated approached the Devaney Paper Company and gave them an offer "they couldn't refuse." The vice-president of marketing for Stillwater made the call and offered to visit the Devaneys in person. The brothers were willing to meet with Stillwater, but remained cautious. "We knew something big was up," Tom was to say later, "but we didn't know what. The offer came as a shock to all of us."

The Stillwater Offer

When Sandy Premus, vice-president of marketing for Stillwater, arrived at the main plant, he insisted that all four brothers sit in on the conference and that no other members of the company be present. This raised both hope and alarm on the part of Tom and his brothers, but they readily acceded to Stillwater's demand for secrecy and confidentiality.

Sandy started right in without any preliminaries. He appeared to the Devaneys as a man bent on a mission: the Stillwater representative was direct and blunt.

"The Stillwater Corporation has had a successful and profitable relationship with the distributors of the Devaney Paper Company for over 10 years. But we don't have a direct relationship with Devaney itself; it's always been 'arms-length.' Now we want to change that. Forever. For a company our size, it no longer makes sense to buy through distributors. We want the Devaney Company to change its policy. We want your company to sell its paper products to us directly.

"Here's why. Presently, Stillwater pays $356 per ton of finished paper product to your designated distributors that goes into making our greeting cards. Since we have distribution plants spread around the country, it means Stillwater has to deal with at least fifteen different distributors representing

Devaney around the United States who then all turn around and buy from one source: you, the Devaney Paper Company here in Massachusetts.

"What does that mean for us? Higher costs because we pay for the 7% distributors' mark-up, more paperwork for us and for you because of the extra distribution layer, and slower turnaround time because of the middleman. It's foolish. We want that practice to end—immediately.

"I don't know how big the Devaney Company is. You're privately held. But let me take a guess what we mean to you, since we spend millions each year buying Devaney paper products from your distributors. I'd say Stillwater represents 15–20% of your total annual dollar revenue. That makes us your premier *indirect* buying customer. That also means you depend on us for a good portion of your profits."

Richard Devaney interrupted, almost shouting. "You're not even close, Sandy! You've come up with some wild number to make Stillwater seem much more important than it really is. Don't give yourself so much credit. We'd never let you become that important to us. It would give you too much leverage!"

But, inwardly, Richard was shaken and tried hard not to show it. Stillwater represented in excess of 10% of the Devaney Paper Company's revenue and was, by far, their most important client. On that score, Sandy was astute and absolutely correct.

"Look guys," Sandy countered, "I know you'll never tell me what percentage our business is worth to you, but it's no secret we're your number one client. Your own distributors tell us that. Whether it's 20% or 15% or just 10%, what's the difference? We're big and you need us.

"Now here's why I came all the way to your offices here in the middle of nowhere to tell you. I have been authorized by the Stillwater president to increase our business to you by 10% *immediately*, that's one-zero percent, gentlemen, and all you have to do is start selling to us direct. That's right. Direct. The distributors don't do a lick of work for the 7% mark-up they're getting and we want to put the profit they're currently receiving where it belongs, in the Stillwater company, because we're ready to take over the full distribution function for you. From your plant to the retail shelves.

"Stillwater would get distributor pricing, plus volume discounts because of our economically efficient order levels. Our computers would simply network with yours and you'd have all the shipping information you would need. It'd cut down on paperwork, selling effort, telephone calls, traveling, etc., and save you money while it was saving us money.

"Besides that, we have offered you one of the sweetest deals on record. You'd be crazy not to do it. We're offering to increase our business with you by 10% immediately and who knows where it could go from there. An offer like that comes through once in a lifetime. Once!"

Sandy looked at the Devaney management team. They returned his stare. No one blinked an eye.

The Devaney Response

Finally, Terrence Devaney, the oldest brother and chairman of the board, said, "We've had a policy of never selling retailers direct for more than 40 years. We've been loyal to our distributors and they know that. They appreciate that loyalty and have brought us many new customers because they trust us not to go behind their backs. They're the ones who sell for us. We don't have a sales force. Never have. Don't intend to."

Sandy was quiet at first, then responded slowly, "Maybe it's time you got yourself one. You're totally dependent on your distributors. Buying direct is something every retailer or card company like ourselves wants to do. One-step distribution cuts expenses, improves efficiencies, and means lower costs at retail for consumers. Everyone benefits. Everyone.

"I want to be heard clearly by all of you in this room," Sandy thundered. "The days of Stillwater working through distributors is over. Over! We refuse to be held back by a policy started by your father that no longer makes any sense. No disrespect to your family, but your distribution concepts are outmoded. They're history! Do you think that Kmart and Wal-Mart buy their large volume purchases through distributors? Sears? J.C. Penney? You folks are all dreaming. You're being left behind because you hold onto has-been business practices."

Tom Devaney cleared his throat and spoke up, "What happens, Sandy, if we don't play ball with Stillwater? What happens if we say 'no'?"

Sandy appeared somber. "We'll pull the plug on all the business we give the Devaney Paper Company through your present wholesale distribution system. Every last penny. We've already lined up another paper supplier just in case you don't agree to these terms. There's no negotiating. That's what we want. You have 48 hours to decide. I hope our offer of a 10% increase in order volume, plus an integrated computer purchasing plan, will entice you to do the right thing. I'm counting on it." With that, the Stillwater vice-president picked up his papers, put them in his attaché case, shook hands all around, then left the board room and the building to his waiting limousine.

Stunned, the Devaney family members sat silently not daring to say anything to each other at first. After several painful minutes of quiet anxiety, Michael Devaney, who had kept quiet during the entire meeting with the Stillwater vice-president, spoke up now. "Do we have a choice? The man was emphatic: Stillwater will pull all of their business with us immediately if we don't agree to sell them direct. Maybe it's time we did. Maybe we are behind in the sophisticated business world of New York and Chicago. Central Massachusetts suddenly feels very isolated from the rest of the world to me."

Richard spoke next. "We've always had a special relationship with our distributors. They trust us. They've been loyal to us. How can we turn our backs on them now?"

Then it was Terrence's turn: "I say forget Stillwater. Sure they're important to us, but don't business ethics count any more? Loyalty? Commitment? We've been working with wholesalers on an exclusive basis. They're among the closest friends we have in this business. To turn against them, why, we might as well put a scarlet 'A' on our chests." Terrence rose to go.

Tom stopped him. "Wait, I know this is an emotional issue for all of us. But the man gave us a business proposition, not one based on emotions. It's not some personal challenge to our family or ethnicity or religion. It's strictly business, Terrence, strictly business. And we need to respond to Sandy Premus and Stillwater using our judgment as businessmen. Do we react like some hotheaded rookies who simply lockstep in place because their folks decided to set up their business a certain way and we refuse to ever consider changing things? We need to look at this coolly. Calmly. And use our heads.

"Now what are the pros and cons that we face?"

SECTION SEVEN
Promotion

Case 7.1
The SlideMakers Company: Struggling to Stay Alive[*]

Time to Celebrate

The three founding partners of SlideMakers, Inc., Stamford, Connecticut, were celebrating their 10-year anniversary of being in business as of June 1, 1998. Dale Huttings, Jonathan Barnes, and his wife, Courtney (disguised), were in a festive mood. They had "beaten the odds," overcome stiff competition, and their company was now considered the number 1 slide production facility in both southwestern Fairfield County, Connecticut, and Westchester County, New York, bordering Fairfield County just to the south. Their revenues were closing in on $1,000,000 and their staff, including the three partners, had grown to seven full-time people.

Looking Back

Joining them in the celebration was their marketing consultant, Larry Myers, who had been working closely with the company since 1990. Myers, a business professor at a nearby university, had been introduced to SlideMakers' management through a mutual friend who had said she was close friends with Courtney Barnes, the vice-president for marketing and finance. "Larry," the friend had asked, "give Courtney a call. This company has a lot of talent and know-how, but they're dying. They do a great job of making high-quality presentation slides for industry, but hardly anyone has heard of them. Maybe you can help."

Toasting the three successful owners of SlideMakers, Larry Myers reminded them of how far they had come since he first had given them that fateful call. "I phoned Courtney in the late spring of 1990 and the three of you seemed ready to close your shop. Now look at what you've accomplished. You're all riding high."

Dale retorted, "I remember that first meeting very well. You told us your fee for putting together a business plan and for pointing us in the right direction. It nearly cleaned out our checking account. And we had plenty of creditors knocking on our doors for money! The three of us felt we were literally betting our very last dime on a marketing consultant we hardly knew. It took guts on our part and it required us to put a lot of faith in you."

Jonathan added, "It's true. You did help us survive those early years, but here we are ten years later and new computer software technology may yet drive us out of the slide production business. What's your answer to that, Mr. Consultant?"

---

[*] All names are disguised.

Before Larry could respond, Courtney said, "Whoa, slow down Jonathan. Today is for celebrating. Tomorrow we can start worrying again about how to stay ahead of the technology curve. Let's just be thankful we got this far."

Back to Partying

The three partners and their consultant were enjoying a local chardonnay and a white clam pizza to celebrate the occasion. They were joined by about two dozen well-wishers who had been invited to the tenth anniversary party in recognition of the company's start-up.

As the party was breaking up, Courtney was reminiscing about how hard it was to get the company up and running. She was directing her remarks to Larry Myers. "All three of us, Dale, Jonathan, and myself, had previous slide production experience before establishing SlideMakers. That's how I met Jonathan in the first place. We were both working for the same slide house and started dating. After we were married, we figured we could make a go of it on our own.

"We asked Dale to join us because of his terrific computer hardware and software skills. It was a wise choice. Each of us brought something unique to the business. Our skills didn't overlap very much. Dale knew how to convert clients' slides from their own computer software programs to ours or he made up the slides they needed from scratch depending on the client's sophistication with computers.

"Jonathan's skills fell into place once Dale handed off the computer output. No one else knows how to produce such high-quality presentation slides at the right price like Jonathan does. He's tops in the business. Me? I handle incoming client calls, contact new prospective clients, and take care of the finances along with our bookkeeper, Jackie. We all work well together."

"You may have worked well together," Larry Myers was saying to Courtney, "but I recall my first visit with the three of you rather vividly. You all seemed so beat, so down. You were all wondering if you were going to have to close the business."

The Marketing Problem

The financial situation for SlideMakers during its second year of business was one of stagnant revenues and costs being pushed up by inflation. Margins were getting tighter and tighter and the partners discussed reducing their draw out of the business in order to pay their most pressing bills on time.

The marketing consultant believed when he first met the SlideMakers' management group that a business plan was their first need and it had to be addressed immediately. SlideMakers did not have a close working relationship with any particular bank in the area and they could certainly use one. An open line of credit up to $100,000 would help the company immensely because of the ups and downs of monthly revenues. The slide production industry appeared to be seasonal. January–May was a busy time, then demand started to drop off in June followed by a very quiet July and August. Once Labor Day was over, things started to pick up again in September with October and November again a very busy period for the company. After the first week of December, however, the company might as well have closed up. There were almost no orders for slides from roughly December 10 to the end of the year.

The three management members all seemed hard-working, committed, and very capable. An informal survey of their computer hardware and software did not indicate any real gaps in slide production technology. Equipment used for duplicating slides appeared adequate with an update on the processing speed of the machinery due the next year.

Competitive Review

Larry Myers suggested a thorough competitive review might help to pinpoint the marketing problem. Courtney Barnes provided enough details about SlideMakers' three main rivals (company names are disguised) that the consultant decided he did not need further independent research to verify Courtney's perceptions.

Competitor 1:
King Graphics. Primary location was New York City with satellite operations in Stamford, Connecticut, and Parsippany, New Jersey. Acknowledged as the industry leader; although dollar volume put them number 1, their production staff shied away from difficult client requests and they routinely handed them over to SlideMakers as long as SlideMakers promised not to divulge who actually did the slide production work.

Competitor 2:
Planetary Graphics. Located in Stamford and Norwalk, Connecticut. Specialized in producing slides for small- to medium-sized firms; did little corporate work. Quality was inconsistent but prices charged for slides were the lowest in the area.

Competitor 3:
Slide Works. Located in Norwalk, Connecticut, the company occasionally made forays after SlideMakers' clients but the company's owners did not seem to have the technical knowledge necessary to really be competitive. From what Courtney had picked up, the company always seemed to be flirting with Chapter 11 bankruptcy.

From what Larry Myers could ascertain, SlideMakers had at least the same or better high-quality, high-tech equipment that its competitors had, such as IBM, Apple Computer, and Harvard Graphics. SlideMakers was competitive with speed of output, turnaround time, and quality.

Pricing

The only critical area where SlideMakers was not competitive was in its slide pricing strategy. Courtney explained, "We have to cover our costs. While revenue remains inadequate to give us much breathing room, we need to charge higher prices than King or Planetary Graphics just to survive. We can't simply give our slides away. We do the best job in the business, in our estimation, and clients often appreciate that. Not all of them, to be sure, since some clients buy only from the lowest cost supplier. That business we don't get. But by and large, companies will pay our price because they know they can depend on us for service."

Service Is Critical

"And that's what the slide production industry is all about. Service. If a top executive needs slides for a big sales or marketing presentation one month, one week, or one day from now, all they want to know is: Did the slides get done on time and accurately? Do you think price matters during crunch time for the president of GTE? Or Xerox? Or Exxon? They all have their headquarters in Stamford and when they need slides, they mean they need them *right away*. Yes, their purchasing department makes sure we don't wildly overcharge them, but when it comes down to the issue of are the slides going to be ready or not, SlideMakers always comes through. We've never let a major client down. Even if it means staying up all night with absolutely no sleep, we're ready to do it and we've done it plenty of times, believe me. We know we're in a service business and it's great service we offer to all of our clients.

"And you know what the sad thing is? We could work really hard time after time after time for a big corporate account, and their attitude stays the same: What have you done for us lately? Heaven forbid, if we miss a deadline or make mistakes when producing their slides, they would have no compunction to go to King Graphics and give them all their business. Why? Because of one mistake. On one set of slides. It's a pressure business and we have to shine all the time. There's no saying to the client, 'Oops, we're sorry. Forgive us. We'll do better next time.' It's always us having to prove ourselves. Each slide order at a time. I tell you, it takes its toll on all of us. We get frayed nerves and gray hair providing slide production services for our clients and a good number of them never bother even to say thanks after we've saved them from near disasters. They just expect us to deliver. And I guess that's the name of the game. We have to hit a home run every time for them or else we're out of the game."

Research

Larry Myers asked Courtney what customer research the company had undertaken. Not surprised at hearing there was no database at all concerning their clients except for a confidential client list (many small businesses usually overlooked this helpful tool), Myers suggested at least some initial research to determine if clients were satisfied or dissatisfied with SlideMakers' service time frame and the quality of the slides.

To determine client satisfaction levels, the marketing consultant designed a simple questionnaire that clients could complete in under five minutes by checking off closed-response, quantitative-style queries. In order to motivate faster turnaround and complete answers to all the survey's questions, SlideMakers promised to hold a drawing from among all those respondents who sent in their finished questionnaires. Three "lucky" winners were to receive $100 gift certificates to one of the area's best restaurants. Since SlideMakers occasionally developed film for the restaurant's owner, the gift certificates were bartered for film development, thus significantly lowering the actual cost of awarding the three $100 gift certificates.

The survey results based on a 70% return rate were considered seminal information to SlideMakers' three owners. Of those clients who gave the company high satisfaction ratings, more than half also noted that SlideMakers' prices were "high" to "very high." Most surprising, though, was almost one-third of the survey's respondents had not used SlideMakers frequently because they were not quite sure what SlideMakers did or of what their services consisted. Thus, SlideMakers was considered the number 2 or number 3 supplier, often of last resort, since little was known about the company's capabilities.

Conclusions Drawn

After analyzing the research data, Larry Myers called the management team together to present the results. He reviewed client concerns over price and the "awareness gap," as he referred to it, that SlideMakers was suffering compared to some of its competitors.

However, Dale Huttings was not impressed. He said, "What do you mean by an 'awareness gap'? We advertise in the Yellow Pages in both Fairfield and Westchester Counties. Most of the new clients we get come to us through those ads. It costs us nearly $2,000 a month for our Yellow Pages' display ads and listings, and since we don't have a full-time salesperson, the Yellow Pages has always seemed like our best bet. How could clients not know about us? When they open up the Yellow Pages, how many companies do you think make quality presentation slides in this area? Not many. And our display ad is just as big as King Graphics."

Courtney had a strong opinion about SlideMakers' price list. "I've told you before, Larry, pricing is not the real issue here. It's service. People will pay whatever they have to pay to get the best service. Something's got to be wrong about the survey. Maybe we sent the questionnaires to the wrong client list. Maybe we should send out another round of 50."

Then Jonathan chimed in, "I never was in favor of using a survey in the first place. If our revenues aren't high enough, we just have to work that much harder for word-of-mouth to finally help us out. The word will get out there eventually."

The marketing consultant looked around the room and listened attentively as each partner spoke. Then it was his turn again. "You all called me in to help you get more business. You've told me you have the best people on staff producing the highest qualilty slides in the area.

"You've convinced me you have the best equipment and computers you can afford to buy at this point and your competition comes to you to bail them out when they have complex, technical jobs to complete. There's nothing your competition does better, but several of them are underpricing you currently. Although this doesn't seem like a big deal to you, since you say service is everything, some prospective clients are staying away due to price. I don't doubt these survey results.

"Another thing. You want more revenue, but the only way you reach out to communicate who and what you are is through the Yellow Pages. I know you can't afford a salesperson to go knock on doors all day long to drum up business, but I have a hunch there are some important folks out there in the corporate world who don't know you exist, or if they have heard of SlideMakers, they don't know very much about you. Actually, it's more than just a hunch, it's right there in the research. Fully one-third of the clients you told me to send the survey to and who responded let us know they aren't sure of the services SlideMakers provides. What do I have to do to convince you there's a real problem here?"

The Words Sink In

Slowly, Dale, Jonathan, and Courtney came around to Myers' way of thinking. Their resistance to the survey's results was softening and they agreed perhaps they had been too set in their opinions to consider other ways they could market the company and price their slide production services.

At this point, Larry Myers bore in on the partners. "Look," he said, "you have to do more than just rely on the Yellow Pages. Yes, it generates business for you, but it doesn't seem to be enough to keep your business afloat. You need to promote yourself more. You need to increase awareness of not just the SlideMakers' name, but all of your slide production and film development services as well. How many people know what you do? Based on what we learned from the research, I'd be worried if I were the three of you. I'd be real concerned. But let's look at the other side of the coin—you also have a real opportunity. If you're as good as you say you are, and satisfaction levels with your work seem solid according to the survey, then getting the word out to area companies is an absolute must."

Myers thought he had scored some points until Jonathan interjected, "I don't like the idea of lowering our prices permanently for producing slides. Not one bit. It just makes it look like we're reducing our quality in order to cut costs. It's going to hurt our image. Do you see Mercedes reducing their prices? Or Tiffany's? Or Rolex watches? If we discount our prices, we'll never be able to charge regular prices again. I'm convinced it's a risky move."

Then Courtney chimed in, "We don't have the money to advertise. Do you know what a display ad would cost in the *Stamford Advocate* or the *Norwalk Hour*? Those are the two biggest daily newspapers in this part of Fairfield County. Then there's Westchester County. How could we afford to advertise in all those newspapers?"

Larry Myers was quiet for a moment. Then he replied, "Businesses don't use newspapers to reach other businesses. It would be inefficient and yes, I agree with you, very expensive. As for pricing, we can do it selectively. Perhaps not across the board. We need to strategize around that.

"Whatever you plan on doing, though," he said, "do something. Plan, think it through carefully, weigh your options, then act. To do nothing will mean wasting your money on hiring me and you surely will sink below the waves. Yes there's risk, but there's risk also in doing nothing. Perhaps more risk than acting and moving ahead. It's a shame you are all so bright and capable when it comes to producing slides, but you know very little about how to market your service effectively."

The three owners looked at one another. They were not used to being confronted this way. Dale seemed ready to say something, then stopped. What exactly were they supposed to do?

Time for Celebration?

Jerry Silvester was looking over recent company bank statements as well as the projected 1999 P&L and balance sheet. As vice-president and minority shareholder of the Arbor Fabrication and Manufacturing Company ("AFMC") in Arbor, Westchester County, New York, he was excited to see the company's equity line debt dropping below $200,000. At the current payback rate, the equity line could be paid off entirely within the next three years. This would mean the partners would be able to increase substantially their salaries from the business, something Jerry felt he needed to do to pay for the upscale personal lifestyle he had chosen for his family.

However, Kym Arnold, president and majority stockholder at Arbor Fabrication, was frustrated and even angry at her partner, Jerry. She felt the company had reached a critical crossroads, one that would determine the very nature of its future success. Kym wanted to *borrow*, not pay back, money from their equity line in order to increase the company's revenues through more business-to-business advertising. Jerry, disagreeing, believed the company would be better served by investing minimally in its operation and spending any extra dollars they had on prospecting for new clients in the tri-state region of New York, New Jersey, and Connecticut using more intensive personal selling techniques.

Personal History

AFMC was incorporated in New York state in March 1990 as a spin-off from the Arbor Tool Company. Kym Arnold was able to register the company as a "minority-owned business" in order to get a better opportunity to win public and private contracts in the construction industry as a female CEO in the metal fabrication industry.

To understand AFMC, one needs to go back more than 25 years to when Kym and Marty Arnold were first married in the late 1960s. Marty did not think the corporate world was for him so he decided to buy into a going business that could use his mechanical ability. The couple responded to an ad in *The Times* placed by the owner of a small appliance fix-it shop located in Arbor, New York, less than an hour from Kym's parent's house, where Marty and Kym had been staying. At first, Marty was put off by what he saw when he went for his initial visit to the shop: inexpensive vacuum cleaners and toasters in various states of disarray and dismemberment were strewn all over the floor. But something caught Marty's attention just when he was ready to leave—several construction tools lying on the floor near the back door.

---

[*] All information including the names are disguised.

Marty asked the owner what the construction tools were doing in an appliance shop. The owner responded that various electrical and building contractors brought their broken tools in to be fixed because they didn't know where else to go. The shop owner farmed out the broken tools to a contact he had in the Bronx who fixed the electric- or hydraulic-driven saws, hammers, generators, and pumps. Marty sensed the business opportunity waiting to be seized and agreed to buy 50% of the business for $15,000 cash.

Hard years of total concentration, sacrifice, and long hours followed. As soon as Kym could, she also helped with the business and contributed to its enormous growth.

Refer to Appendix A for Arbor's financial results from 1975 to 2000 (forecasted) and to Appendix B for a comparison of gross revenue dollars, profits in dollars, and number of staff employed by Arbor Tool since Marty bought into the business.

The original name and nature of the company, Jack's Fix-It Shop, had long since been changed from the days Marty had first seen opportunity lying on a concrete floor in 1975. Marty had wisely sought out the leadership of the construction trades in New York City from both the management and union sides and had slowly convinced CEOs, shop stewards, purchasing agents, and job foremen alike that Arbor Tool would be the most dependable and efficient source around the tri-state region for construction tool repair, new tool purchases, and all the many accessories needed by the building trades for their work.

Marty and Kym, after buying out the original owner of the fix-it shop back in 1977, had successfully ventured into military and energy utility contracts, international exporting of U.S.-made tools, and the importing of specialized high-quality European construction machinery.

The Spin-off

By 1990, Arbor Tool was doing so well it almost seemed as if it were running on "automatic pilot." Marty was losing interest in running the company anyway; he said he'd rather go fishing any day than spend it working. However, the entrepreneurial spirit that had gotten them this far had not quite gone away for Kym and she talked excitedly that year about a new project she was seriously considering.

Both electrical contractors and the Brotherhood of Electrical Workers had approached Arbor Tool from time to time to see if the owners would be interested in fabricating certain materials needed for job site work. Arbor had many capabilities but metal fabrication was not one of them. Yet the thought of getting into metalwork was intriguing because one of Arbor's biggest competitors, Harrison Suppliers, had a fabricating division that was said to be quite lucrative. In fact, Marty suspected Harrison was getting some extra tool volume at Arbor's expense because Harrison was making so much money on fabrication they could cut their tool profit margins to become more competitive.

Marty and Kym conferred on what to do next. Marty felt that Arbor needed full attention from only one of them; Kym could start up a spin-off from Arbor Tool if she were so inclined to begin to learn the metal fabrication industry. Kym jumped at the chance. She conducted some cursory research and decided that the new company would concentrate on making electrical brackets first, and later on, specialty electrical junction boxes for the construction trades in New York. Not wanting to go it alone, she sought partnership with someone who could handle outside sales while she took care of the new company's finances, order fulfillment, employee development and internal paperwork. They would share the engineering and production supervision.

Kym had trouble finding someone she considered to be a compatible person for a partner. After searching fruitlessly for more than ten months, she agreed to meet someone recommended by an acquaintance who managed an electrical supply house in New Jersey and who was looking to leave that situation for an ownership position in a small business. That "someone" was Jerry Silvester, and while he seemed to come across to Kym as a "typical New York area macho guy," he also seemed amenable to partnering with Kym and generating the investment Kym felt was needed from a junior partner. Besides, Marty had met Jerry, too, and the two of them got along quite well together, sharing fishing stories that got funnier and wilder each time they met.

So it was that the Arbor Fabrication and Manufacturing Company was created; issues like how to divide stock ownership, what starting salaries would be, job responsibilities, and the like were all ironed out after some arduous and sometimes heated negotiations. Arbor Tool would supply some of the financing and bank connections, whatever technical know-how and contacts Marty could offer, plus some surplus office furniture. Other than that, AFMC was pretty much on its own.

The Learning Curve

Kym soon realized the fabrication industry was much more complicated and competitive than she had first bargained for. There were several dozen large national companies that provided metal fabrication to thousands of buyers domestically and globally. AFMC would never begin to compete with them. What the company needed were niche products, fabricated metal parts that the local construction trades could get from very few vendors. However, even though Jerry had excellent networking connections among a strong list of prospective customers, several would-be buyers backed out when they realized the company was just starting up. Fortunately, several old-time Arbor Tool customers agreed to start buying from AFMC. The breakthrough came, though, when the New York Port Authority placed their first order for specialty brackets. Later, AFMC was able to get into the custom order electrical junction box business and create even more awareness of their presence.

The specialty boxes were made from one of four materials: black steel, which would then have to be painted or galvanized to resist corrosion; stainless steel; aluminum, which could also be painted at the buyer's request; or pre-galvanized metal sheets. Customers requiring these boxes would specify material, size, corrosion resistance, the number of holes needed in the junction box, and the type and color of paint for the box exterior.

AFMC rented fabrication and office space about a mile from Arbor Tool and began in earnest in mid-1990 to make and sell their brackets. The junction boxes followed in late 1992. Their progress in the intervening years had been substantial, but lately business had stalled and Kym was getting very concerned. It wasn't an issue of getting new customers; the issue for Kym was some basic philosophical differences with her partner, Jerry.

Tough Decisions Ahead

The revenue stall the company was experiencing at the $2.5–$3.0 million level was not because of a lack of customers. Kym felt they could possibly bring in more orders but the type of business that was out there required more advanced computerized machinery than AFMC owned. In fact, AFMC had never owned state-of-the-art machinery. The company had adopted a policy of only purchasing second-hand fabrication equipment in order to hold down the partners' capital investment in the business. This meant production snafus from time to time that dearly hurt their reputation and credibility. In an era of "just-in-time" parts and materials, electrical contractors were ordering their junction boxes with very little "wiggle room" to spare. Any delays in producing and delivering the boxes could cause severe dislocation and expensive downtime. AFMC, like its competitors, had to deliver their product on time or face angry customers who did not want to hear excuses about missed deadlines.

Kym believed revamping the shop's machinery would cost the company $350,000 but could be repaid within 8–10 years using some bank financing. Mostly she wanted to use internal company funds if she could to avoid costly interest fees. Kym thought they could pull it off if the partners each took out considerably less income for 3–5 years. The newer machinery meant the organization could seek out and acquire new business and better serve its current customers. This really upset Jerry.

Jerry believed Kym was looking at the problem from the wrong perspective. He thought the best approach would be to invest at most $10,000–$15,000 in prospecting new customers in the New York City area and continue to just get by with the machinery they had. Yes, the revenue curve had flattened out, but the way to grow was not through "pie in the sky" thinking on Kym's part and the very risky purchase of untested, new machinery for the shop floor. Rather, Jerry felt they should continue going after the same specialized junction box business, and simply expand their current customer base by trying to take customers away from competitors such as Harrison Suppliers.

Added to Jerry's list of negatives was Kym's idea of reducing their take from the business to help pay for the machinery purchases. For Jerry, the prospect of taking a cut in his partnership draw was a non-starter. He and his wife had relocated to Darien, Connecticut, from Staten Island within the past year and their monthly living costs had soared.

A final consideration was the building where AFMC was physically housed. A critical long-term issue was space. If the fabrication business grew beyond the $3.0 million level estimated by the year 2000, AFMC would literally run out of space to store, cut, trim, bend, weld, and paint all of the brackets and custom-made junction boxes required by their current clients. In addition, the gas and electrical lines first installed in the 1940s from the street to the building seemed about at their peak delivery capacity. Running at full steam on two 8-hour shifts was not possible in case more business came in the door; the utility lines simply could not handle that kind of load.

Kym and Jerry, along with several real estate brokers, had been searching for new space for the past six or seven months. There were some promising new sites available in Arbor, with several options on, near, or well away from the river, but their rental costs would increase by at least $25,000 per year for several of the larger and more modern facilities. That would put a damper on updating machinery, expanding their marketing efforts, putting together better employee benefit packages, or making increased interest payments to the bank in case of higher interest rates.

The two partners were now at loggerheads. Following blow-ups between the two of them that simmered for days, it was clear that Kym and Jerry had reached a paralysis in decision making because neither one of them would compromise with the other. When Kym approached her husband, Marty, for advice he responded with, "Arbor Tool is keeping me happy and gives us a nice lifestyle. You were the one who was really excited about getting into fabrication, not me. You're the one who decided Jerry was going to be your partner, again, not me. Not to sound mean, but you've got a business partner in the fabrication industry and it isn't me, it's Jerry."

Upset by what Marty had said, and faced with Jerry's intransigence, Kym was having trouble putting together a strategy to get Jerry and her off dead center. She considered her next move . . .

APPENDIX A
Arbor Tool Financial Results 1975–2000(est)

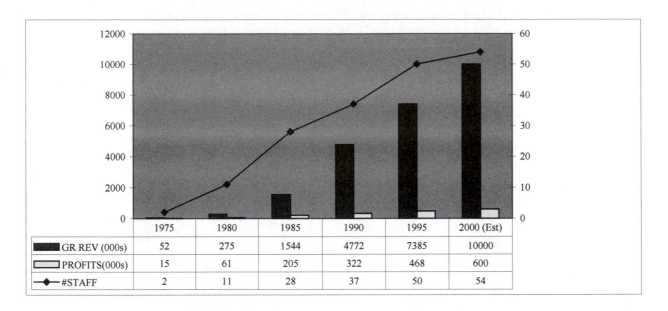

	1975	1980	1985	1990	1995	2000 (Est)
GR REV (000s)	52	275	1544	4772	7385	10000
PROFITS(000s)	15	61	205	322	468	600
#STAFF	2	11	28	37	50	54

APPENDIX B
Arbor Tool Biannual Results 1990–2000

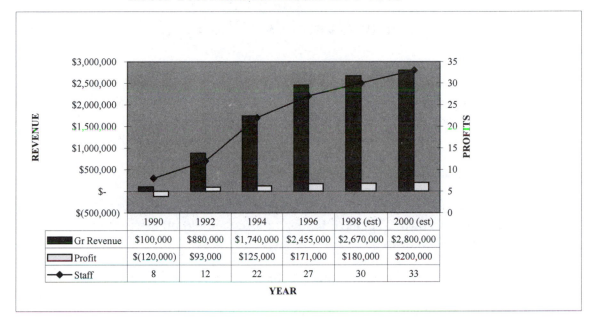

	1990	1992	1994	1996	1998 (est)	2000 (est)
Gr Revenue	$100,000	$880,000	$1,740,000	$2,455,000	$2,670,000	$2,800,000
Profit	$(120,000)	$93,000	$125,000	$171,000	$180,000	$200,000
Staff	8	12	22	27	30	33

YEAR

Case 7.3
Procter & Gamble's "Cheery Monsters"

Seth Gramby felt good about himself. At 22, he had completed an economics major in college and a marketing MBA at an ivy league university. He was offered six different starting positions; Seth chose Procter & Gamble in Cincinnati, Ohio, over the rest because, as he said to his parents, "It's like getting your doctorate in marketing only you get paid a heck of a lot of money while you're learning!"

Seth's First Assignment

Seth showed up for his first day of work and was suitably impressed by the new buildings P&G had constructed in downtown Cincinnati, having vacated their old offices at 6th and Sycamore since the company had long ago outgrown their previous space.

He was told he would be assigned to the Cheer Detergent Brand Group, Packaged Soap & Detergent Division. Seth had no particular preference for detergent over the soap, paper, or foods divisions, so he felt starting out as a brand assistant on one of America's best known brand names was a good omen.

Seth was introduced to the brand manager, Tom O'Keefe, and the two assistant brand managers, Lorinda Holwell and Skip Loskins. He was shown to his desk and promptly told by Tom to spend the next two to three days reading background consumer research for the brand. "It's the best way to start, actually," Tom explained. "You can't claim to know your brand unless you're familiar with how consumers perceive the product itself. Don't speed read through it. Take your time. Learn about the brand and the packaged detergent category."

Seth took Tom's philosophy to heart and spent two solid days reading through the voluminous material gathered on Cheer detergent since the brand's U.S. national introduction in 1951. Top-loading clothes washers were all the rage and Cheer was formulated especially for those machines. A white color-based detergent with speckled blue and green particles, Cheer had earlier used the slogan "Gets your clothes whiter than white" to emphasize its cleaning power.

Repositioned towards the end of the 1960s, Cheer switched advertising agencies and its product slogan became "All Tempa-Cheer" to reinforce its all-temperature cleansing ability in hot, warm, or even cold water. Cold-water washing became popular 30 years ago when imported oil prices went from $5 to over $30 per barrel. Consumers wanted to economize wherever they could, and avoiding the use of hot water when washing clothes had been considered a definite plus.

Competition

Seth's brand group was located not very far from the behemoth of all detergent brands: Tide, the Cheer brand group's fiercest competitor in the multi-billion dollar detergent product category. Tide had been P&G's first brand entry into the modern, post-World War II era of detergents specially formulated for top-loading clothes washers. "Tide's in, dirt's out!" had been the brand's slogan seemingly for generations and U.S. consumers had made Tide far and away the number 1 brand in the industry. Cheer, in contrast, was a distant, but still important, number 2.

The detergent category was dominated by three international companies, two headquartered in the United States and one in Europe. The U.S.-based corporations were Procter & Gamble and Colgate-Palmolive. The European company was Unilever and the world was their battleground where the three global corporations along with numerous smaller players all fought for shelf positioning, increased package facings, and dominant consumer "share of mind." It was considered especially important for brands to become part of the buyer's "evoked set." Research showed the large majority of all detergent shoppers knew the brand they wanted to purchase before entering the supermarket. Brands not in the consumer's evoked set could only hope they could get the buyer's attention at the very last moment as they stopped their carts in front of at least a dozen different, competing detergent brands. Couponing, price discounting, rebates, contests, premiums, and other sales promotion tools were constantly being used to attract cross-over, nonbrand loyal consumers or to keep wavering brand loyalties intact.

Seth's Responsibilities

As brand assistant on Cheer, Seth was informed very early on by Skip Loskins, the junior assistant brand manager, that he would be responsible for "crunching the numbers" on the brand, initiating sales promotion ideas, and being the brand's representative at various meetings with sales, manufacturing, procurement, planning, I.T., and other key functions.

As the most junior person on the team, Seth was expected to do the "skut work," just like Skip and every other marketing manager did before him as they entered the P&G culture as brand assistants. The company had a strict hiring code: Everyone started at the bottom and promotions only came from within. You earned your way up the ladder, position by position. By the time you got to the top, you were a Procter employee through and through with more than 20 years international marketing experience behind you.

Seth learned how to "crunch" like every other brand assistant. He spent a great deal of his time producing 18-month rolling forecasts of manufacturing requirements for Cheer for the top 40 U.S. SMSA markets, by package size, by month, aggregated by quarter, half year, and year. Tedious work, yes, but an important way to understand how to translate national sales forecasts into actual product for the "Try Me" sample, regular, giant, and family size powdered detergent cardboard packages and liquid plastic containers.

Seth also became adept at analyzing Nielsen share reports and it became his task to turn around receipt of the share report into a brand progress report within 24 hours. These share analyses were considered so important to the Packaged Soap & Detergent brand groups that every brand assistant was expected to do whatever s/he had to do to get the report out promptly and accurately. For Seth, that meant staying up until 3 a.m. to make sure Tom O'Keefe had the report on his desk as quickly as possible the day after share figures were available.

A Break in the Math Action

Seth yearned for something more creative to do, some way he could contribute to the brand by completing a project that could use some of his nonmath skills. It's not like he didn't like math and numbers; it's just Seth yearned to exercise more than just the left side of his brain while at work.

His first big chance came when he received a call one morning from Sonya Zwikowski in the Premiums department. "I understand you're the new brand assistant on Cheer. Am I right?" Sonya asked. When Seth answered in the affirmative, Sonya continued, "Our job here in the Premiums area is to help brands identify sales promotion opportunities. We service all the company's brands, but I'm assigned specifically to Packaged Soap & Detergent. Since you have the responsibility for Cheer's sales promotion activity, do you mind if we talked a bit about your brand?"

Seth jumped at the opportunity, sensing this would be more to his liking than just using his MBA to develop manufacturing and inventory requirements. He agreed to meet Sonya after lunch the next day in the Premiums section of the building. When he got there, he was surprised and exclaimed, "Look at all the premiums scattered about your office! There must be hundreds of different items here."

Sonya laughed and agreed. "Yes, I have a hard time throwing anything out and they pile up quickly. You wouldn't believe how many hundreds of companies approach this department every year trying to sell us some new premium idea they've developed. They're smart, though. If a P&G brand picks up one of their items, with our marketing coverage and muscle, it could mean a lot of bucks for the premium supplier. We're typically their number 1 target. So I get to see every salesperson in the business and they always leave samples."

Seth rejoined, "With all the premiums you have here, how do I start picking out some concepts? And how do I know a premium would be compatible with our brand and target audience? Cheer doesn't usually sales promote with premiums according to our brand manager. This could all lead to a blind alley. And besides, we'd have to test market it, too."

"True enough," Sonya responded, "But don't you think it's worth a try? I have pre-selected a group of twelve premiums for you to look at because I think they each have high consumer perceived value for the cost involved to us. Every brand is looking for an edge. Every brand assistant is looking to get promoted. It's in your interest to put some time into this effort."

Seth grunted his acknowledgment and started to look over the premiums that Sonya had selected for him to review. Duz detergent had had a long brand history of including premiums in every box they sold, something like the toy "prize" in Cracker Jacks candy. However, Cheer did not share that history and Seth was leery of trying to convince his product manager to use premiums at all. After looking through the assorted hand towels, cook books, games, small toys, key chains, and other items Sonya laid out before him, Seth was convinced premiums would not be in Cheer's immediate future. He was plenty busy with other brand activities.

As he rose to leave Sonya's office, something green and blue with streaks of red and spindly legs sitting on one of her shelves caught his eye. "What's this?" Seth asked.

"Oh, it's something that just came in. It's a rubber toy for little children. We're assured by the vendor it is nontoxic, won't choke a small child because it's too big to get down their throats, and is resistant to children trying to tear it apart. That would give it high marks for durability and safety, wouldn't you say?"

Seth held the toy in his palm. He didn't know it at the time, but he was holding the future "Cheery Monster" premium. It would involve his time, thought, and much of his energy for the next year.

(Refer to Appendix A for Seth's hand drawing of the "Cheery Monster.")

Research Was Next

Seth took several samples of the toy back to the product group and asked Tom, Lorinda, and Skip what they thought. Skip spoke up first, "Waste of time," he whiffed and walked out of Tom's office. Lorinda was kinder. "I've got three small children. Why don't I give this thing the 'kid test?' If they like it, you'll have at least something to go on." Tom nodded his assent without adding anything of his own to the brief meeting. Well, Seth thought to himself, at least the idea wasn't turned down out-of-hand. Perhaps something will come of this.

He had forgotten all about Lorinda's "kid test" until the next morning when he checked his voice mail. The third message was Lorinda's. "Seth, I can't believe it! My children loved the toy! Seriously, this is something you should see through. It seems like a winner." Excited, Seth called Sonya Zwikowski on the phone and asked to meet with her immediately. "Wait a minute!" Sonya laughed, "I've got meetings scheduled for the next three hours. How about some time after lunch?"

"How about lunch? I'll buy," Seth countered and Sonya agreed. Sitting in a nearby restaurant enjoying their lunch, the two discussed what the next steps were in the process. "Well," Sonya started, "you just can't depend upon one premium, you know. We need to pick out at least a half dozen premium possibilities and put them all through a consumer test panel. Then we'll see how the toy matches up against these standard premium items and also how it does against some historical data we keep on premium items which then went on to become very successful for their brands."

"How long will all this take?" Seth wanted to know.

"We can set up the consumer panel pretty quickly. We have a list of women head-of-households aged 25–39 who all live nearby with at least one child living with them under six years of age. They're prescreened and willing to come into our research facility, for a generous fee of course, so all we have to do now is get on the panel's schedule. All in all, about a month I would estimate."

"Fine, sounds great. Tell me what the research will cost and I'll include it in the brand's budget once I get the official okay from my supervisor," Seth said. "Put Cheer on the schedule and I'll confirm Tom's approval as soon as I can." A day later, Seth had the go-ahead in writing and confirmed it with Sonya. "It's a go, Sonya, and here's hoping we have a winner."

Confirmation

Buried under a grueling workload which necessitated alternate Saturdays and even sometimes Sunday hours at work, Seth soon forgot about Sonya and the panel. However, about a month later, he saw an e-mail from Sonya. "Yes!" began the message, "The little rubber toy you refer to as your 'Cheery Monster' was a smashing success. Congratulations! Not only did it come in first in the consumer panel member's rating forms, easily outdistancing the other five premium items, it also was the third highest scoring premium ever, according to the director of the Premium department. Let's get moving right away!"

Seth was stunned with this outcome. He had had confidence in the little toy right from the start, but the third highest score ever? This indeed was important news. He forwarded Sonya's e-mail to the rest of the brand group and then thought about his budding future at P&G. A successful sales promotion event, something that really caught everyone's attention in the division, would be a tremendous boost to his marketing management career at the company. Seth was truly excited for the first time since he had started on the Cheer brand group the past February and envisioned, in the not-too-distant future, being promoted to assistant brand manager and then brand manager. He would be known as the "Cheery Monster" guy. The one who started his ascent through the ranks based on a gutsy call with a children's toy. *Yesssss!*

Some Options

Seth considered the range of options the brand would have in promoting the toy. Based on Purchasing department estimates that each Cheery Monster premium would cost six cents to manufacture and ship to Cincinnati from sources in Asia, Seth decided the offer would be three "free" Cheery Monster premiums for each giant size box of Cheer purchased by the consumer.

Referring to the brand's P&L, he noted each incremental box of Cheer sold through to consumers provided another 75 cents to the brand's bottom line. True, the use of the premiums would reduce this net operating profit contribution by 18 cents, netting 57 cents per giant size Cheer (not including promotional expenses); however, this appeared to be a very efficient means of obtaining extra business and building brand share nationally. The entire brand group concurred.

Seth wrote a brief analysis of each option that came to mind, regardless of whether the consumer bought a cardboard box or plastic container. Note: the cost estimates did NOT include the cost of the three Cheery Monsters.

1. **Mail redemption:** Ask shoppers to buy one container of giant size Cheer, send in the UPC symbol from the label along with an order form to get their three free Cheery Monsters in the mail. Neat and clean with no impact on the Manufacturing department but it meant dampening impulse purchasing

by the parents. Having to wait for two–three weeks for the toys would discourage some buyers. Instant gratification would be lost.

Estimated Incremental Sales: 200,000 units.
Costs: 75 cents to mail the three premiums to consumers including postage, packaging, and handling.

2. **Inpack:** Place the premium inside the box of detergent and put a large, sunburst announcement on Cheer's front panel announcing the toys. It doesn't change the packaging but it does involve a change in the production line. Also, good artwork will give mothers an idea of what's inside, but inside *is* inside. Buyers would not be able to see the premiums until they got home and opened the box.

Estimated Incremental Sales: 500,000 units.
Costs: Upwards of $1.30 per container to place each of three premiums inside its own plastic package to prevent the toy from touching either the powdered or liquid detergent, putting the premiums inside the container before filling, plus Manufacturing's "learning curve" costs that would involve machine down-time and training assembly line workers.

3. **Onpack:** Place the premium outside of the box using some type of shrink-wrapping operation. Certainly this was common enough in the consumer packaged goods industry, but it could be entirely new for P&G. The downside was the cost and effort to shrink-wrap, but perhaps an outside vendor could do the job. Plus, were the premiums really secure from theft? Could or would shoppers use sharp items to cut through the shrink-wrap material and just take the premiums? On the plus side, the premium would really stand out and cause a lot of consumer excitement and impulse purchasing. No need to have to wait for the premiums in the mail or wonder what they really looked like inside the detergent package.

Estimated Incremental Sales: Minimum 750,000 units.
Costs: $1.75 to shrink-wrap the cardboard box or plastic container by an outside vendor. Extra cost of 45 cents due to only being able to ship 9 containers of detergent per case instead of the usual 12 units per case.

4. **Nearpack:** Forget putting the premium inside or on the box. Instead, develop a point-of-purchase ("p-o-p") free-standing display already containing the Cheery Monsters that could be set up in minutes.   Seth would have to negotiate with the Sales department, but he felt a cash incentive provided by Sales to the store managers could help "guarantee" the display piece would be left up at least one week, maybe even two, if the product group was lucky. A downside was getting retail support and the chance a sizeable number of stores would not cooperate with the promotion.

Estimated Incremental Sales: 600,000 units.
Costs: $25.00 per display each holding 300 Cheery Monster premiums to be sent to 8,000 retail outlets.

5. **Internet?** Seth could not immediately conjure up a way to use the Internet for the promotion, but he felt there might be some advantage to continue the process of considering the Internet or other options before he made his final choice.

Choosing One

Seth carefully considered each of the five "premium delivery" choices he had generated and then decided to discuss both onpacking and inpacking with Manufacturing in Ivorydale, P&G's huge plant operation located about 10 miles away from downtown Cincinnati. He was concerned about how the Manufacturing managers assigned to Cheer detergent production would react to something that could greatly complicate their lives. Mail redemption, nearpacking, or using the Internet would have no impact on Manufacturing so he left those options out of his discussion.

At the meeting, to Seth's surprise, the Manufacturing folks were receptive to both inpacking and/or onpacking. Said one, "We do it for Duz detergent all the time. Inpacking is no big deal as long as the volume taken up by the premium does not prevent us from filling up the standard amount of detergent inside the box. In no way can we ship boxes lighter in actual product weight than it says on the front panel. It's illegal, plain and simple. We purposely overfill right now to avoid any chance we could underweight. Underweight boxes would be a public relations disaster as well as a violation of law." Everyone agreed and the Manufacturing representatives promised they would make several sample boxes and plastic containers of Cheer with the premiums inside to ensure enough detergent could still be placed into each package to satisfy the stringent net weight requirement.

Now for the onpack concept, Seth thought. No one could remember ever shrink-wrapping a Procter product. However, that did not seem to dampen their enthusiasm for the idea. Seth pointed out his preference for onpacking by saying, "I know it's a risk because some shoppers may just want to slit the shrink-wrap and take the premiums without paying, but to me, putting the Cheery Monster premiums on the outside of the box creates the potential for a lot more consumer excitement and impulse purchasing due to the strong stimulus of actually being able to see the premiums. The children are going to go nuts when they're in the cart being wheeled around by Mom or Dad. Can you imagine their reaction when they see the Monsters?"

Satisfied he had made his point, Seth asked, "What do you all think in Manufacturing? Can you do it? Is it possible?"

The response around the room seemed positive, but definitely guarded. Procter apparently had no shrink-wrapping equipment and no one seated at the table had had any prior shrink-wrapping experience. However, they were reluctant to say no, either. Everyone seemed to want to please Seth because his interest and energy for the project appeared so intense.

The Manufacturing personnel at the meeting made no commitments, but they promised to look into the possibility of shrink-wrapping and advise the Cheer brand assistant as to their findings. The investigation would take at least two weeks and maybe longer. Seth agreed to their time parameter and held off any further action on the premium concept until they got back to him.

It's a Go

Nearly a month had gone by. Seth was getting antsy and wondered if all his efforts so far behind this sales promotion premium concept would yield any personal benefit to him. His promotion to assistant brand manager might just have to depend on other things he had accomplished for the brand since the Cheery Monster project was stalled.

Then he received a helpful call. The voice on the other end of the phone was excited. It seemed there was an existing shrink-wrap operation within a half-hour of Ivorydale and initial contacts with the owner of the shrink-wrap machinery had been extremely positive. Procter wouldn't have to buy any capital equipment, just ship several dozen cases of detergent and hundreds of Cheery Monster premiums over to this outside facility to test the shrink-wrapping part of the process. It would be an initial run to see how well the shrink-wrap machinery worked and how tight the fit was around the premiums and the detergent box or plastic container.

"There's another issue, though," the voice from Manufacturing was saying to Seth. "The added bulk of the premiums would mean Manufacturing could no longer get twelve giant size boxes or plastic containers of Cheer inside the standard heavy cardboard outer case package that protects the boxes of detergent during shipping from Procter to the wholesaler, then on to the retailer."

"How many can you get?" Seth asked.

"About nine without causing any stress on the boxes."

So, Seth thought, another obstacle in my way.

However, this adjustment in units per case did not prove to be a critical sticking point because the Sales department had no objection to the change in case count. Other than slightly higher costs for increased outer case packaging, Tom O'Keefe had no problem with it either. Seth was relieved. Everything seemed to be falling into place.

Time for a Decision

A lot was riding on the success of this sales promotion effort and Seth knew it. Seth had to show some unusual spark, something truly different from all the other brand assistants to move up through the ranks. He wanted the Cheery Monsters to be his lever to get his first promotion at P&G as well as become his legacy for the Cheer brand.

APPDENDIX A
Cheery Monster
(Size: Approx. 1.5" high, 3" wide)

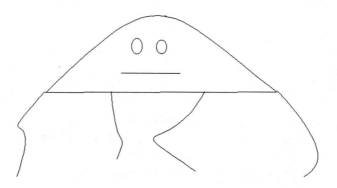

Case 7.4
Sherwin-Williams' Advanced Superpaint:
Too "Super" for Its Own Good?

Market Introduction

The publicity releases emanating from the Sherwin-Williams Corporate Headquarters building in downtown Cleveland were extremely upbeat. The company, whose logo showed an inverted, open container of paint pouring its contents over the earth with the words, "Cover the Earth," was announcing its latest technological advance: "Duration" one-coat paint. With annual sales of over $4 billion worldwide, Sherwin-Williams' management had reason to gloat; no one else in the very competitive paint industry had a product anything like it.

However, Dennis Robb, one of the company's sales managers who was headquartered in the northeastern region of the United States, was not as upbeat. "Oh, Duration paint is amazing," he was saying, "please don't misunderstand me, but the claims the company is making about this product are leaving some paint contractors and consumers a bit incredulous. In fact, they simply don't believe the paint can do all we say it can do and therein lies our problem. We are trying to market a product that people simply don't believe can perform up to the company's advertising claims."

The Test Market

Sherwin-Williams had tested their advanced paint product in four different locations around the country during 1998–99. Referred to as "Advanced Superpaint" in test markets and now renamed "Duration," the product had received fairly solid consumer acceptance over the past 12 months. Price resistance, a real concern to the company, appeared to be minimal.

One glitch, however, had occurred in Florida. Sherwin-Williams tested a campaign theme promising such high performance and consumer satisfaction that both paint *and* labor were guaranteed. If the paint turned out to be defective in any way, Sherwin-Williams would cover the entire cost of repainting the surface, not just materials. Professional paint contractors reacted very angrily to this and word spread fast through the Internet. Tempers flared. The way the contractors saw it, Sherwin-Williams was making it easier for "fly-by-night" paint contractors to take business away from more established firms. Why? Because now anyone could guarantee their work by simply saying, "If you don't like it, Sherwin-Williams will do it over—at no cost to you, the consumer, for both paint and labor." Whatever edge the more experienced contractors had over newcomers to the industry, according to this reasoning, could evaporate if Sherwin-Williams persisted in this type of promotion.

Not wanting to alienate the contractors, Sherwin-Williams pulled its advertising and promised not to repeat the offer in any other state or upon national product launch. This was considered especially unfortunate, however, to the Sales department. They had believed the guarantee would strongly differentiate the company from its many competitors and make the introduction of "Duration" an even greater success.

To many investors on Wall Street before the introduction of Duration, Sherwin-Williams seemed to have lost its leadership in product development to other paint manufacturers that had caught up in resin and titanium technologies. Company management anticipated that Duration would soon change that perception.

Would the company once again regain its dominant role in the paint industry? Was Duration, market tested as "Advanced Superpaint," the answer . . . or not?

Background

The original Superpaint, created nearly 20 years ago, was considered in 1982 to be the perfect product to differentiate Sherwin-Williams in the premium high-end paint segment. R&D advised Marketing that the product could be safely positioned as the best, most durable paint available both to contractors and the general, do-it-yourself ("DIY"), consumer market.

Sales and profit results had been excellent nationally, but curiously, not nearly so in the northeast region or the west. Benjamin Moore, with under $1 billion in annual sales nationally, had the number 1 market share position in the northeast and Kelly-Moore had the edge in the western region.

Current Share Information

Share data for mid-1998 supplied by Dennis Robb showed the following line-up.

National Brand Share of the Residential Home Market

Sherwin-Williams	20%
Benjamin Moore	14
Behr	06
Kelly-Moore	05
Sears	05
Dunn Edwards	04
Glidden	04
Dutch Boy	03
All Other	39
Total	100%

Sherwin-Williams' share problems in the northeast stemmed from the fact that although they had remained a strong number 2 to Benjamin Moore in the contractor segment, the company had slipped to the number 3 position behind Benjamin Moore and Behr (the featured Home Depot brand) with the DIY segment. Home Depot had approached Sherwin-Williams several years ago with an interest in stocking the company's paint products; Sherwin-Williams' management decided it was not in the company's best interests to sell directly to the heavy price discounter because it might disrupt retail sales in their other locations. In contrast, the Behr Company saw the opportunity to expand their own retail sales significantly through Home Depot and successfully negotiated a close working relationship with the giant DIY-oriented retailer.

Reviewing the Marketing Mix

Product

The company firmly believed Duration had exciting product benefits never before available in interior or exterior house paint products. Recent product head-to-head (or, perhaps more relevant to the industry, "wall-to-wall") competitive usage and attitude studies conducted in selected homes all around the nation suggested R&D had a strong winner.

Duration could claim to be equally successful as both an interior and exterior paint, but Sherwin-Williams' management decided to launch the product as strictly an exterior paint for the time being. As an exterior paint, Duration had such penetrating power due to its small molecular structure that there was *no need to prime bare wood* before applying the product. It went over any color in a *single coat* and, finally, Duration could be applied safely in temperatures *as low as 50 degrees*. This new product was so good and technologically advanced, marketing executives were frankly worried about the company's credibility. Would contractors and consumers believe these claims? Would the product—over time— actually perform as well as R&D said it would?

Distribution

Obtaining shelf space for new company products would never be a problem for Sherwin-Williams because the company had over 2,200 company-owned or franchised stores located throughout the United States. Duration was to be made available only in Sherwin-Williams' locations, thereby giving the stores exclusivity over sales of the product during its introductory phase.

Price

Sherwin-Williams' Superpaint, the forerunner to the new Duration, retailed at under $27 per gallon for both interior and exterior flat. Exterior satin sold for a little more, but typically retailed for under $29. In contrast, Duration retailed between $33 and $35, a cost premium for the user of roughly 25%. This was a real concern to the company; Home Depot sold Behr paint for under $20 a gallon and, despite low *Consumer Reports'* evaluations, Behr and Home Depot were doing excellent business.

Test market results showed some, but not substantial, buyer resistance over this higher pricing level. The company's executives believed there was enough extra value in Duration that the higher price level was acceptable to most consumers and that the product line would continue to show increases in total unit sales.

Product line cannibalization, another large concern, apparently was not occurring to any noticeable degree. Superpaint sales were actually increasing, albeit more slowly, as Duration was being introduced around the country. This would suggest the demographics for Superpaint and Duration were different enough so that buyers for each price level of paint were in different income groups. Or possibly, users of Duration were looking for different benefits and were willing to pay the 25% premium price differential.

Positioning

Another issue vexing company management was how to position this new paint to best advantage. Executives were concerned about over-promising, yet they knew their technological lead would once again dissipate over time as competitors analyzed the chemical composition of Duration. The opportunity window was open to Sherwin-Williams for a relatively short period; time was not necessarily on the company's side and modesty over what this paint product could accomplish certainly would not become it.

Promotion

Most recently, the company had promoted its regular Superpaint product using animated humor. A woodpecker was shown trying to chip his/her way into a home painted with Superpaint; its only "reward" was having its beak badly bent from all its futile efforts.

Sherwin-Williams had not tipped its hand yet on how it would promote its Duration formulation. And one overriding worry remained: would customers really believe the claims that the company seemed to be prepared to make? And, did it make sense to introduce Duration at a time in company history when contractors and the DIY segment all reported they were perfectly satisfied and happy with Superpaint?

SECTION EIGHT
Marketing Strategy and Planning

Introduction

Roger Longrelle, marketing manager for the Moreau beer brand (disguised) in the United States, was excited about the prospects for Moreau beer sales for the rest of 1999 and on into 2000. The Moreau Brewing Company finally appeared ready to make a major move into the United States beer market, a strategy which Roger had long supported but which had languished at Moreau headquarters in Quebec, Canada.

Background

Moreau Brewing was one of Canada's flagship brands. Although temporarily displaced as a leading Canadian brand in 1994–1996 by its arch enemies, Molson and Labatt, Moreau was once again a leading contender "north of the border" by 1997. Closely associated with such Canadian symbols as the maple leaf, ice hockey, clear blue skies, and endless plains of snow covered land, Moreau was proud of its Canadian heritage. Heavily favored by men 16–35, Moreau Brewery was an institution in Canada and a proud national symbol.

Heretofore, the U.S. market was never seriously considered prime territory for Moreau. The beer did well in "spillover" areas such as Michigan, New York, and Maine, but for the most part Moreau Brewing management had pretty much ignored the U.S. market. Roger believed it had something to do with the conservative, nonrisk-taking profile that top executives had followed for generations, and also quite possibly because the marketing group did not wish to take on such branded giants as Budweiser and Miller.

That all changed in mid-1997. The two families that owned Moreau decided to sell a majority share to a consortium of European and Central American investors who promised to invest considerable amounts of money in the company and expand its global reach. Rather than treat the U.S. market as an afterthought, the new president and the vice-president of marketing advised Roger and his marketing group that Moreau would gear up for an invasion of the United States "that would make the crusades look like a picnic." Bold words coming from Quebec, but the gauntlet appeared to have been thrown down and it was going to be an all out war for the consumer's share of mind.

Roger's Dilemma

The Moreau USA marketing team immediately began a series of focus groups and segmentation studies so that they could obtain more insight into the U.S. beer market and the kind of drinker most open

---

* All names and other information are disguised.

to switching their beer brand loyalty from such brands as Budweiser and Miller to Moreau. The focus groups were held in upstate New York and in Detroit, two markets where Moreau beer more than held its own against the likes of Budweiser.

The results were interesting, but since these were compiled from just a few initial focus groups, Roger knew the data would need further analysis. Following are several highlights from the focus groups' verbatims:

Moreau Positives	**Moreau Negatives**
• Good beer taste, refreshing • Consistent quality, fresh, doesn't disappoint • Image is male-oriented, associated with sports and athletes • Can be substituted for Budweiser; just as good • Thought to be a premium beer	• Has higher alcoholic content than Budweiser or Miller • Costs more than other premium beers • Not my first choice for beer, but definitely in the refrigerator • Don't buy it for parties, just for myself

As Roger reviewed the focus group results, he was glad to see Moreau was considered as good a beer as Budweiser, the number 1 brand by far in the United States, for both taste and its ability to refresh the drinker (refer to Figure 1). However, Roger was also upset to note that participants had wrongly perceived that Moreau was higher in alcoholic content and in price versus U.S. beers when, in fact, that was not true.

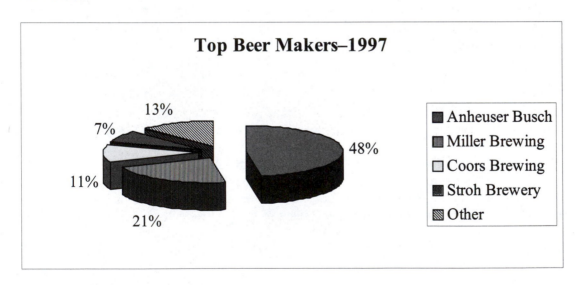

Source: Market Share Reporter. Gale research, 1998

Figure 1.

Adding to Roger's concerns was the lack of identification of Moreau with Canada. The beer sported a maple leaf and made no attempt to hide its cultural roots in all of its promotional communications.   Yes, it was a fact that television spending was low and the brand depended mostly upon radio and instore point-of-sale advertising, but how could men in New York and Detroit not identify Moreau as an imported beer? When pressed by the focus group moderator, several men had come forth with an association of Moreau beer with Canada, but the majority of men did not know or care.

However, this Canadian national identity *did* matter very much to the new owners of Moreau Brewery, who all felt that imported beers in the United States commanded more respect and a higher price profile with American drinkers. Products such as Beck's, Amstel, Molson, and Corona had found extremely profitable niches for themselves among a better-educated, higher income, white collar segment of male drinkers 21–45. Perhaps just as important, this product class was also attracting more and more females who were trading up from "premium" beers like Budweiser and Miller to imported brews. Moreau's advertising agency had been advised by top management to develop a pool of commercials that emphasized Moreau's Canadian heritage. The belief was Molson had built its reputation and brief number 1 share position on being Canadian; when it had strayed from this position, its market share and sales had declined. Now Molson was back to being "Canadian."

The question for Roger, then, was should he support top management's belief that Moreau should be known as an imported, Canadian beer and copy Molson's approach, or should he push back against management and recommend the brand stand on its own as simply a great tasting beer that people should try as an alternative to Budweiser? Did Canada really have cache as a beer exporting country, or was Canada perceived to be so much like the United States that it just did not matter to American drinkers whether the beer had such a heritage?

Next Steps

Roger knew he had to tread very carefully around this positioning issue. His supervisor, the vice-president of marketing, felt the brand should be presented as imported, Canadian, premium, male-oriented, and associated with hockey. Roger believed this would play well in border states where Moreau was already strong. But what of the rest of the United States? Compared to "rust belt" states, the southern tier states had much less interest in hockey, a lot less knowledge and interest in Canada, and consumer research showed significant resistance to spend more for *imported* alcoholic products like wine and beer. Indeed, focus groups in Atlanta had already confirmed Roger's worst fears: male participants had been candid in their assertions that they didn't care much for Molson or Amstel ("or other European fancy, dancy stuff that costs a lot but doesn't give you much") and "things Canadian" did not impress them. Roger assumed the same attitude would be present all through the south, southwest, and perhaps even through portions of the midwest and west central.

Roger needed to make a decision that would impact the brand for years to come. How could Moreau stay Canadian when most drinkers south of the country's border did not care about its pedigree? And wouldn't Moreau be making a mistake by trying to share the same Canadian positioning as Molson?

On the other hand, Roger felt top management's support of associating Moreau with Canada and hockey would definitely play well among northern border states, both in strong markets in the north central and northeast, but probably the northwest as well.

Roger dithered. He was at a loss to figure out how to meld the two approaches together to satisfy Moreau management, yet speak effectively with a highly focused campaign to the consumer.

Case 8.2
Argone-Phelps: Who Will Win the Battle . . . and the War? *

Insurrection

Katlyn O'Callaghan looked at her watch once again. Only two minutes had passed since she had last noticed the time. Gosh, I'm really nervous, she thought to herself. As she waited outside the CEO's office, Katlyn felt real misgivings about why she had been called in to see the president of Argone-Phelps Exhibition Company, a division of a European-based conglomerate.

Argone-Phelps has disparate interests around the world but concentrates its efforts mostly in Europe and North America. An important activity is its Trade Exhibition group, which conducts industry trade shows and major exhibitions. Argone-Phelps runs such trade events as jewelry, golf equipment, books, travel, boat, aerospace, and tool manufacturer shows in order to bring providers face-to-face with their direct-buying customers. Depending on the type of exhibition, these customers could be other manufacturers down the line in the manufacturing process or wholesalers, retailers, and service providers like travel agencies. The general public is not invited or allowed to attend these strictly business-to-business exhibitions.

So what Argone-Phelps does basically is find suitable convention space in key markets, create a plan for how to apportion the space to fit manufacturers' needs who wish to exhibit their offerings, then use direct mail to target prospective attendees who are motivated to see the latest developments in their industry. Argone-Phelps generates substantial revenues both by charging the manufacturers for the rented space in the convention hall as well as by selling tickets to the attendees to gain admittance to the show. Argone-Phelps, in effect, brings manufacturers and prospective buyers together in the industrial marketing arena similar to the way retailers bring manufacturers and consumers together in the consumer market.

The CEO, Eric Cutler, came out of his office and motioned for Katlyn to join him. Once inside his office, Katlyn tried to maintain a calm outer demeanor, but lost a bit of her control when Eric closed the door behind them. "Uh oh," she thought, "maybe I'm being fired." As vice-president, senior manager of the Chip and Electronic Manufacturers Equipment Show—known by its acronym "Cemes" (pronounced as "Seams") around the industry—it was Katlyn's responsibility to oversee the work of 25 Argone-Phelps' employees to run the Cemes event four times a year. The show was one of Argone-Phelps' prime events and netted the company in excess of $10 million annually.

Eric started with, "Katlyn, I can't sugar coat this news to you although I've tried to think of ways to ease the disappointment. I've decided just to tell you flat out."

---

* All information including names are disguised.

Katlyn tried to show no emotion but she could feel her heart beating up against her chest. "It's okay, Eric, you've always been straight with me. Go ahead, I'm prepared for it." What Katlyn braced herself for was to hear for some inexplicable reason she had lost her position with Argone-Phelps Exhibition Division. What Eric Cutler said next completely floored her.

"Your stewardship of the Cemes event has been terrific for the past four years. It's grown in size, and revenues have grown accordingly. Cemes represents a disproportionately large amount of our profitability here at the division. So what I've just heard from one of my sources in the field deeply disturbs me." Eric paused to draw in a breath and to take a moment to reflect on what he was about to say. Katlyn sat immobile, unable to do or say anything until the CEO finished his monologue.

"You and I have both discussed over numerous occasions some of negative feedback we've received from several of the manufacturers. Their marketing executives have made some angry comments to our salespeople over the past two years concerning the fees we've been charging providers to rent space. And they think the cost of ticket prices for attendees is too high. They have also complained about the peripheral expenses exhibitors must pay for food, security, and parking, which all generate a lot of extra revenue for us."

Katlyn interrupted, "But Eric, those complaints were largely confined to our San Jose, California, venue. Our customers in New York, Atlanta, and Dallas where we put on the same Cemes events the other three times a year have never really complained much at all. Maybe they haven't all been as satisfied as we would like, but it's been only the San Jose show where we've had the most problems."

"Well," Eric responded, "that's exactly where we face an insurrection of sorts from some of those dissatisfied manufacturers. I've just heard a rumor that several of the largest chip and electronics manufacturers based on the west coast have banded together, along with the American Chip and Electronics Manufacturers Association, to put on their own Cemes show cutting Argone-Phelps out entirely."

"They can't do that!" Katlyn exclaimed. "They would never succeed without us! We're the industry leaders, the people with all the convention know-how. We're the ones who conceived and started the Cemes shows around the country. How dare they! Who's part of this conspiracy?"

"At this point I frankly don't know," Eric said as he shrugged his shoulders. "It could be anyone. Maybe some of the biggest hitters in Silicon Valley. We need to find out. Fast. They're going to go after key executives at Sony, Motorola, IBM, Apple, Dell, and Compaq. The list of possible defections to our own show suddenly seems endless. I hate to think about it, but we're vulnerable, Katlyn. Really vulnerable. I wouldn't have thought it just a few months ago, but I think we've underestimated just how angry some of the exhibitors have gotten. To mount their own show in cahoots with their industry association is a terrible threat to us. It's not just our image. Yes, yes, our image could be hurt terribly and that could have real ramifications for us in terms of our credibility with other high-exposure national shows. I understand our image is important, Katlyn. I'm not discounting that at all. But that's some long-term strategic stuff we'll have to deal with."

The Short-Term Effects

"Short term, we need to look at the bottom line. If we lose out to these up-starts, we could lose the Cemes show in any of the other three venues, or heaven forbid, all of them. Then, like dominoes, some other shows could be lost. The profit hit would be enormous. Enormous! We have to draw the battle lines right now and right here. We cannot lose the Cemes show in San Jose. I don't care what you have to do or how much it costs, within reason, but save the show! Save it, Katlyn, because saving it means you save your own job, my job, and dozens and dozens of other jobs around here."

Katlyn was quiet for a moment. "Eric, I'll do my best. You know that. However, I would like to point out one thing. For the past year I've been concerned over the San Jose show and I've told you how I've felt about the booth prices being increased year after year until some of the exhibitors were squealing like pigs caught under the proverbial farm gate. Well, the chickens, so to speak, have come home to roost. I need a free hand, Eric. I don't want to have to come back to you and ask permission to do everything that needs to be done, piece by piece. If you trust me to save the show, then delegate the decision-making authority to me as well. For the really big decisions, I'll try to come to you first, but back me up on this one, Eric."

Eric nodded his head in agreement. "Fair enough," he said, "but don't get carried away with concentrating just on San Jose. They're going ahead with their own show one way or another. We want to win this battle, for sure, but don't lose sight of the fact we have to win the war and the war may have several separate battles along the way. Strategize carefully as if this were a war, not just one encounter."

Katlyn smiled, but said nothing. She rose, shook Eric's hand, then left his office. If there was one thing Katlyn was ready for, it *was* a war.

Next Steps

Katlyn called an emergency meeting of her Cemes team and requested they stop whatever work they were doing and attempt to gather as much information as they could from trusted sources on the San Jose "insurrection" as she referred to it.

Within 24 hours, Katlyn and her team had learned from a confidential source within a company that had already been approached to bolt the Cemes show that the new competing convention was going to take place two weeks *after* Cemes. That meant a real time press for the new show group since Cemes was just three months away.

The venue was going to be the same: San Jose, California. Of critical importance, the cost per square foot to any exhibitor that elected to skip Cemes and sign up with the competing group had been lowered from the Argone-Phelps level of $40 down 50% to just $20 per square foot. Katlyn made an immediate decision. "We'll match it. Let's call every single one of our exhibitors who has signed on for the San Jose Cemes exhibit and tell them we've just saved them some big bucks. That should help stem at least some of the prospective defections."

The contact refused to provide any more information.

Katlyn faced a myriad of complex decisions with scant information. She knew, however, that the battle between Argone-Phelps Exhibition and the upstart association/manufacturers ad hoc group would be won or lost on two fronts: which exhibition group could attract the most important exhibitors and which convention the important attendees from such companies as Sony and Motorola ended up going to.

"Plain and simple it's a numbers game," she instructed her team. "We either win it in the trenches or lose it there. Let's construct our plan of attack. First, we'll start with the attendees. We've already struck a blow with the reduction in provider cost per square foot charges down to $20 so let's hope that move works in our favor over the next week or two."

Ticket Sales

Attendees to the Cemes event come from a wide spectrum of industrial and media sources. Since the key draw to Cemes was to see the latest in chip production techniques and electronic gadgetry, robotics, computer, appliance, and toy manufacturers would be the first pool of prospects. Indeed, any industrial or consumer product that used computer chips and/or sophisticated electronics would provide Argone-Phelps with a prospect organization. Automobile, boat, and plane manufacturers; banks, insurance companies, and other financial institutions looking for better security devices; and consumer electronics providers would be likely candidates.

Media sources include trade newspapers, association magazines, business writers for the *The Wall Street Journal* and *The New York Times*, and independent features writers who were on assignment from newspapers, periodicals, financial investors, and manufacturers. Local cable television usually show up the first day to announce how jam-packed the convention center was to viewers. In return for free access to the exhibition floor, the cable company has always been willing to supply news reporters who gushed about the health and vitality of Cemes.

The main marketing tool used by the Argone-Phelps Company to generate ticket sales for their convention shows is primarily direct mail. Based on years of past exhibition show experience, Argone-Phelps' managers had compiled a confidential database of attendees for each of their national or regional trade shows. These lists are arguably Argone-Phelps' most important assets; by knowing who had attended in the past, the company could avoid having to buy lists and lists of new names for each show and therefore be forced to mail thousands of extra mail solicitations to industry people who might or might not have any interest in attending a specific trade show.

Direct mail is considered a "rifle" medium in that it was sent only to those people who presumably had an interest in attending a specific trade show.

Although Argone-Phelps' management has very efficient mailing lists to go by, and each trade show manager has access to information suggesting which companies would or might be interested in sending their employees to the exhibition, direct mail still had its limitations. Annual employee turnover in some firms approached 25%. Mailings to previous employees were a complete waste of money. Some firms went out of business while new ones emerged that had to be researched and approached about the Cemes show. Budgets changed. Some years a whole department might be encouraged to attend the trade show while in other, leaner years perhaps just 1–2 representatives could go.

Argone-Phelps provided a toll-free "hot line" number in their mailings so prospective attendees could call to discuss the merits of attending the trade show or ask any questions they might have. However, research conducted by the company showed only a small fraction of the direct mail recipients ever bothered to pick up the phone to discuss their interest or ask questions about the show's exhibitors, cost of attending, etc.

Another marketing approach used by Argone-Phelps for some of their larger shows is a personal solicitation call placed by one of Katlyn's team members to department heads of the larger companies that typically sent at least five or more employees to a trade show. These supervisors were given special incentives by the company to increase their attendance at the show. These incentives or "package deals" as they were sometimes referred to included free food coupons, "comped" (complimentary) hotel rooms, and sometimes even free transportation to and from the trade show. Argone-Phelps rarely paid for the complimentary hotel space, plane fare, or rental cars they "gave away" to their key customers since the hotels and transportation companies themselves were glad to provide the company with some free services. Argone-Phelps brought in so much business wherever they held a convention that hoteliers and airline executives routinely provide the company with a certain number of free rooms and tickets. This meant Argone-Phelps can then turn around and hand out these incentives to their best clients.

Katlyn understood that what worked in the past for Cemes was not going to be sufficient now that a competing trade show was going to be shopped around the west coast. She needed more ammunition. Checking her e-mail, Katlyn noticed an urgent message from one of her team members. The e-mail read:

Rumor, not confirmed as yet. Competing trade show to Cemes is being called "Champ." That's short for Chip and Electronic Manufacturer Program. It's hokey, but the acronym is giving the sponsors an opportunity to use the play on words that they will be the "champs" in the San Jose fight with Argone-Phelps over who can win the minds and hearts of the exhibitors and attendees.

Katlyn wanted to brush off this latest indignity and ignore it, but she could not. Imagine, her company going up against the "Champ!" What would these people think of next? It was time to turn up the heat. It was time to go beyond direct mail and a few selected phone calls to make sure Argone-Phelps won this battle . . . and the war.

Case 8.3
Stew Leonard's Dairy B:
The Move to Organic Milk—Are the Risks Worth It?

Stew Leonard, Jr., the CEO of Stew Leonard's Dairy, Norwalk, Connecticut, had just finished listening to a presentation by three MBA students on whether his supermarket operation should consider switching from regular milk to organic milk. "The preliminary results seem positive," he was saying to the students and their course instructor, "but the cost of changing over the dairy operation from non-organic to organic milk will cost us about $3,000,000. I just don't know if it's worth it."

Background

Stew Leonard's Dairy (www.stewleonards.com) is a fascinating study of how to differentiate a business in the crowded, mature supermarket industry. Started first as a door-to-door milk delivery business by "Grandpa Leo," the company was forced to rethink its mission in 1969 when the state of Connecticut used the law of "eminent domain" to take over land used by the family to house its fleet of delivery trucks. Using the cash from the sale of the land as a grubstake, Stew Leonard, Sr., started a small convenience store operation. He stocked just a dozen or so dairy items like milk, eggs, cheese, yogurt, cream cheese, and cottage cheese in his location along Route #1, a busy north-south local road that parallels Interstate #95.

Business was brisk and soon the store expanded, then expanded again 21 times over to where today the Stew Leonard's operation in Norwalk has made the *Guinness Book of World Records* as the store with the fastest moving sales per square foot (roughly ten times the industry average). The store is a regular stopping-off point for businesspeople from around the world to study how the Leonard family developed their marketing strategies. A second store was built in Danbury, Connecticut, in 1991 and a new store opened in Yonkers, New York, in the fall of 1999.

What makes the three Stew Leonard's locations so different from typical supermarkets? First, as you approach the Norwalk site, a visitor notices the "farm" outside the store where goats, geese, ducks, hens, and roosters are entertaining children who might otherwise never get to see farm animals. During the summer, a "hoe down" tent is set up so that families can order and eat meals under a giant canopy. Beside that is a garden shop that sells plants and flowers and an ice cream shop that always seems to be busy with customers no matter what the season.

Inside, the store's traffic flow goes in only one direction starting to the right so that each and every customer passes by every produce offering beginning with Bethie's Bakery (Stew Leonard, Jr.'s sister). Then, the shopper moves on to the dairy area where buyers can see the milk being processed and packaged through giant glass windows. Unique features such as animated, singing characters; a focus on carrying only the freshest meat, fish, fruits, and vegetables; "direct to the customer" pricing; an oversized salad bar; barbecue area; and limited selections (the store does not carry very many staple items) separates the store from its much larger competitors like Stop & Shop, Finast, Big Y, and Grand Union. In fact, customers soon learn that shopping at Stew Leonard's requires going to another, more traditional supermarket for such things as paper goods, pet food, and home cleaning and maintenance items.

One of the key strategic decisions early on during the operation's growth was to attempt to buy in bulk direct from manufacturers rather than go through distributors. The savings would then be passed on to customers as long as they were willing to buy in larger, family-sized containers. This has made the store a favorite of larger families, but the point of some criticism from single people or smaller families who did not wish to buy the larger food and drink containers in the store. Although it has meant disappointing the singles demographics segment, Stew Leonard management has never wavered from its bulk, direct-buying approach.

Another key strategic decision was to private label as many products in the store as possible. The Stew Leonard's brand is dominant throughout the shelves; national brands are brought in just for those product categories in which the Leonards have decided not to get involved such as colas, paper products, and certain condiments.

Consumer Trends

One of the ways Stew Leonard's Dairy has kept track of new supermarket trends is to attend as many industry conventions and seminars as possible while visiting their competitor's stores both here in North America and in Europe, Asia, and South America. Each store visit is written up and the author has to include the "One Best Idea" s/he came away with from the site visit. These reviews, along with customer suggestions that are solicited in the stores themselves, are read each week by key managers for ways the company could increase its customer satisfaction levels and sales.

One such growing trend was the move towards organic products. Alarmed by news reports showing use of old or contaminated meats, fish, and vegetables by unethical store employees, American consumers are becoming wary of just what is in their food and drink supplies. Pesticide use, growth hormones, additives, supplements, and early harvesting has purportedly made much of what we eat virtually useless in terms of its nutrient and vitamin value. This has created a boom in vitamin and herbal remedy sales as consumers have perceived their health may have been compromised by the business practices of corporate agribusiness.

Organic farming is a movement that started as a reaction to this perception of "assembly line" food production and low nutrient values. Organic food must be grown to strict Federal government guidelines as to what actually constitutes true "organic" food. Any farm operation can switch from non-organic to organic food production, but the process takes at least three years before a farm can officially be certified as "organic."

Stew Leonard's built its reputation on the quality and economic price of its dairy products and currently buys all of its milk from an upstate Connecticut dairy farm that has committed its total output to the Leonards. The stores offer nonfat, low-fat (skim), and regular milk to their customers. Due to customer interest and demand, Stew Leonard's brought in a brand of organic milk (Rocky Mountain Products) to see what customer reaction would be like. This gave the stores an opportunity to get into the organic milk business without making any long-term business commitment to sourcing organic milk under its own brand name. However, Stew Leonard, Jr., is considering the possibility of changing the current dairy farm operation over to organic farming if consumer demand justifies the decision.

Contact Is Made

Coincidentally, an MBA faculty member was instructing a course in market research and contacted Stew Leonard's to see if there was a project that required consumer research. It would offer the graduate students a chance to conduct real research while providing the store with helpful information. Stew, Jr., agreed to the idea and a team of five MBA students was formed. Their quantitative research survey is included in the case as Figure 1. They interviewed women, 18–54, who were the primary shoppers for their households and who were regular purchasers of milk at Stew Leonard's (N = 124).

Purpose and Major Findings

The purpose of the research was twofold:

1. To determine whether the respondents had heard of organic milk and what their purchase intent would be.

2. To determine the price elasticity of demand for organic milk given different pricing levels.

The major findings of the research were:

1. Consumers were most concerned over fat content level and taste when purchasing milk.

2. Skim milk and 1% milk were the most popular types of milk products sought.

3. Nearly 50% of all respondents were familiar with organic milk and of those, half again had tried it.

4. Three-quarters of all respondents indicated they were extremely or somewhat interested in trying/buying organic milk.

5. Of those concerned about drinking organic milk, taste and price bubbled up as the main resistance points.

6. Priced at $2.49 per half gallon, 25% of the sample indicated they would shift purchase to organic milk from non-organic milk. If priced at $1.99, there would be a 44% shift in purchases from regular to organic milk. (The price of regular milk in the half gallon size is $1.99 at the time of the research.)

7. Women 40–54 were much more apt to make the shift, with a purchase intent to change over to organic milk much more significant than those aged 25–39.

Conclusions

Based on these findings, the research team concluded that Stew Leonard's could expect at least a 20% shift in overall milk purchases from non-organic to organic once the store offered both varieties under the Stew Leonard's brand name label. The caveat was this shift would occur only as long as there was no differentiation in price between the two types of milk products. A sufficiently large consumer base was already knowledgeable about organic milk so that store management could anticipate product turnover immediately upon offering the organic milk for sale. Other, uninformed consumers would need to be educated about the value of organic milk, but this was not considered to be much of an obstacle. Since one of the main consumer concerns was taste, the MBA students recommended Stew, Jr., consider introducing the organic product with free taste tests for up to one month following product introduction.

Finally, the team recommended product changeover as a long-term goal for the store whether the cartons were labeled "organic milk" or not. Since the store flourished under the banners of "freshness" and "direct to you" market strategies, the shift to make all milk products organically based appeared to be a natural extension of the company's mission.

The CEO's Reaction

Stew Leonard, Jr., seemed impressed with the research team's work and their findings. He was glad to learn that awareness of organic milk was high and that consumers were ready to make the switch from the non-organic side to organic food and liquids.

However, as Stew concluded the meeting, he said, "My competition is slowly including organic milk in their stores, but my research suggests it is still not a big seller. Eventually we may all switch over to only organically grown products, but for now, my organic section is limited to some selected fruits and vegetables in the store we source from various sources. However, milk is a different issue. I would only plan long term on having organic milk sold under the store name here at Stew Leonard's.

"That means I have to make the $3,000,000 commitment up-front to change the current dairy operation from which we source all of our milk products. Since we are putting so much money into our new store in Yonkers, I don't have the financial capability of moving ahead right away on the organic milk project, but given another 9–12 months, this issue will be on the front burner again.

"I'll take under advisement what the research team has uncovered. I recognize how organic milk fits into our strategic vision to offer nothing but the freshest and safest foods to consumers, but the investment required to do that creates real concerns on my part whether it's worth it or not. This requires more thought, perhaps more research, and, at the very least, a careful break-even analysis.

"Let's assume, for argument's sake, that we make the commitment to go organic. Using hypothetical examples, my gross margin on a quart of milk I sell for $.99 is 20%. Based on estimates given to me by my financial people, I can expect my cost for organic milk in the first three years of operation, after the changeover is complete, to cost me at least 50% more than my current milk products. After the third year, I would expect the expense of running the farm will drop to where raising cows on organically grown food will only present a 25% premium. I plan on initially pricing organic milk at twice the price for regular milk—$1.99 per quart. I've price-shopped my competitors and they're selling organic milk for as much as $2.50 per quart. So even when doubling my milk prices I will still be very competitive.

"This pricing scheme doesn't include amortizing the $3,000,000 that I intend to do over ten years. If we sell 5,000 quarts of milk per week in each store, then that's 15,000 per week for the three stores combined. Assuming no incremental sales increases due to introducing organic milk, a rather conservative outlook, what would my profit outlook be if 25, 50, or even 75% of my current milk customers switch over to the organic products? Can I amortize the entire $3,000,000 in ten years and still show a profit? How would that compare with just staying with my current line of milk products and not switching to organics at all?"

Figure 1

STEW LEONARD'S ORGANIC MILK QUESTIONNAIRE

Date: _____   Location: Danbury _____   Norwalk _____

Respondent #: _____   Time Start: _____   Time End: _____

Protocol: Approach every fourth woman entering the store who appears to be between the ages of 18–54. If the shopper is accompanied with someone else, make sure the interview is conducted only with this one shopper. After finishing the survey, count and wait for the next fourth female shopper to enter the store.

Qualifiers:
1) Are you the primary shopper for your household? (check one)

_____ yes, continue   _____ no, TERMINATE

2) Do you shop at Stew Leonard's at least once every 2 weeks? (check one)
_____ yes, continue   _____ no, TERMINATE

3) Do you purchase your milk from Stew Leonard's? (check one)

_____ yes, skip to question #4

_____ no, probe for 3a and 3b, then TERMINATE

   a) Why don't you buy your milk from Stew Leonard's? (Fill in)

_____

   b) Where do you currently buy your milk? (Fill in)

_____

4) In what age range are you in? (Read list and check one)

    _____ Under 18, TERMINATE

    _____ 18–24   _____ 25–39   _____ 40–54

    _____ 55+ , TERMINATE

INTRODUCTION

Hi, my name is _____ and I am conducting a brief survey on milk products for Stew Leonard's. I would like to include your opinions today. Everyone who participates will receive a coupon for a free ice cream cone as our way of saying, "Thank you for your time." The interview will take no more than 5 minutes and your answers will be kept strictly confidential.

I will start off with some general questions about your shopping habits, then proceed to more specific questions. There are no right or wrong answers, just your honest opinions which are very important to us.

GENERAL QUESTIONS

5) Including yourself, how many people live in your household? (check one)

    __ 1   __ 2   __ 3   __ 4   __ 5   __ 6 or more

6) About how much milk do you purchase in a typical week and in what sizes? (Indicate amounts)

    _____ Quarts   _____ Half Gallons   _____ Gallons

7) What kind(s) of milk do you purchase? (Read choices and circle applicable responses)

   Whole milk   Skim milk

   2% milk   Lactose free milk

   1% milk   Other? _____ (Fill in)

8) I am going to show you a card with five characteristics of milk and I am going to ask you to rank them in order of importance to you. Please mention them in order, with your first response being the most important and the last being least important. (Fill in rank order. Rotate order of the three cards to avoid order bias and circle which card was used.)

___ Price ___ Taste ___ Consistency ___ Nutrients ___ Fat Content

Card Used: *1*   *2*   *3*

SPECIFIC QUESTIONS

ORGANIC MILK SCRIPT

SAY TO RESPONDENT: "At this point, I'd like to read you a short paragraph about organic milk."

Read the following: Organic milk is produced by cows that are fed on 100% organically grown food that comes from land not treated with pesticides or fertilizers for at least three consecutive years. It is considered to be free from any "impurities" after that time period. Organic milk is available in whole, 2%, 1%, and skim milk varieties.

9) Were you previously familiar with organic milk? (check one)

_____ No, SKIP TO QUESTION #14

_____ Yes, continue

10) Have you ever tried organic milk? (check one)

_____ No, SKIP TO QUESTION #14

_____ Yes, continue

11) How often do you drink organic milk? (Read choices, circle one)

___ Only once ___ Occasionally ___ Regularly ___ Always

12) Do you notice any differences between organic and regular milk (check one)

_____ No, SKIP TO QUESTION #14

_____ Yes, continue

13) If so, what are they? (Fill in)

_____

14) After hearing about organic milk in this survey, how would you describe your interest in it? Would you say you are: (Read list and check one)

_____ Very interested in purchase

_____ Somewhat interested in purchase

_____ Have no opinion either way

_____ Somewhat disinterested in purchase

_____ Very disinterested in purchase

_____ No response given to question

15) Regular milk is offered at supermarkets in a price range of $1.29 to $1.99 per half gallon. Organic milk is currently being offered by supermarkets at a price range of $2.29 to $2.99 for the same half gallon size. How would you rate the value of this price for organic milk compared to regular milk? (Read list and check one)

_____ Extremely good value for the money

_____ Good value for the money

_____ Neither a good nor poor value for the money

_____ Poor value for the money

_____ Extremely poor value for the money

_____ No response given to question

16) Do you have any concerns about drinking organic milk? (Do NOT read list; circle all mentions)

Bad for your health	Consistency	No nutrients
Price too high	Scam	Spoils easily
Taste	No concerns	No response

17) I am going to show you three separate cards with a price for a half gallon of organic milk. Out of your next TEN purchases of half gallon milk containers at Stew Leonard's, how many units would be organic milk IF it were offered at these prices: (Show cards in descending or ascending order of price. Alternate between the two. Mark down the order.)

ORDER: _____ 1 to 3   _____ 3 to 1

Card #1: $2.99 (circle one) 0   1   2   3   4   5   6   7   8   9   10

Card #2: $2.49 (circle one) 0   1   2   3   4   5   6   7   8   9   10

Card #3: $1.99 (circle one) 0   1   2   3   4   5   6   7   8   9   10

18) What comments or suggestions do you have for Stew Leonard's concerning organic milk possibly being offered at the store?

_____

Thank you for participating! Here is your coupon for a free cone.

SECTION NINE
Internet Marketing and eCommerce

Case 9.1
Provincetown.com: Does Anybody Know We're Here?

Frank ("Skip") Dickerson, for eight years CFO of Mapco, Inc., a $3 billion diversified energy company, was musing about his most recent venture: the purchase of a Web site with the URL "Provincetown.com."

"I wonder where this latest impulse is going to take me," he thought as he looked out on Cape Cod Bay from his office window. "ecommerce is going to continue to expand. You don't have to be a rocket scientist to figure that one out. But for now, Provincetown.com may be one of the best-kept secrets in the universe. How do I grow this darn thing? Can it ever be profitable?"

Background

Skip Dickerson has spent most of his life in the top rungs of corporate life. After practicing law as an associate at Cravath, Swaine & Moore in New York City, he rose to vice-president and treasurer of the Bethlehem Steel Corporation. From Bethlehem, he went to Mapco, which employs over 6,000 people. Skip has had management responsibility for the accounting, treasury, audit, information systems, tax, purchasing, strategic planning, risk management, and credit functions within the company. He has also served as a member of the senior management committee.

Prior to Skip's relocation with his wife to Cape Cod in 1998, he was involved in several software and communications ventures in which he served as an investor, officer, and director. Some worked out; others did not. However, Skip felt each experience was leading him towards a venture with marketing a product on the Internet. So when he and his wife were reading a local Cape newspaper and saw an advertisement offering the domain "Provincetown.com" for sale, he jumped at the chance to try his entrepreneurial hand at running a Web site.

The Web Site in 1998

Started by an assertive and successful female entrepreneur around 1994, Provincetown.com was still struggling to turn a profit by 1998. Skip saw the growth potential in expanding the Web site and paid "a bit more than $50,000 for it. Back in early 1998," Skip said, "I didn't think the Web site had been managed very well. In fact, information was not arranged clearly and navigation around the site was messy and difficult. Although I didn't know anything about Web design, I did have software experience and the notion of owning the site really intrigued me."

Who would operate and design the Web site itself? For this task, Skip turned to Doug Anarino and hired him on as managing director. Doug had had experience as a freelance graphic designer, a production department supervisor for a large publishing company in England, and head of technology for a start-up media company. Better yet, Doug had been raised in Provincetown and had a lot of active business contacts in the area.

Skip also needed a part-time marketing director. Doug had recently returned to the Cape and was a natural in terms of soliciting advertising for the Web site. "I was lucky in finding Doug and his mom because they knew the area well and were friendly with so many local people at this end of the Cape. They've really helped re-launch the site in a very short period of time."

The Web Site Now

With Skip as the owner/business manager, Doug as the daily operations person, and a marketing director knocking on doors for business up and down the commercial areas in Provincetown, the three held out high hopes for reaching financial break-even by year 2000. In order to do this, the Web site would have to generate in excess of $100,000 in revenue to cover expenses such as salaries, payment of fees to their Internet service provider (ISP), and advertising of the Web site in local and Boston area newspapers and magazines.

One measure of the Web site's fortunes was the tracking of "hits" made on any of its Web pages and "unique visitors," a count of each separate person who logs on to the site, no matter whether they visit one or more pages. In January 1999 Skip estimated daily "hits" were averaging 15,000; by July 1999 the hits had increased to 60,000 per day.

Likewise, unique visitors had climbed from roughly 400–500 per day in January 1999 to over 1,500 per day by July of the same year. Advertising clients had increased from a base line of 70 to more than 140 in the same seven-month period. Clearly, things were looking up.

Competition

Skip's Web site was being closely shadowed and mimicked by another Web site with a URL of "Provincetown.net." Skip believed this was illegal because the site came under the usage definition of a ".com" enterprise, but since no one was really policing the Internet very closely for this kind of sham, Skip felt he could do little but ignore his local competitor and hope the site would fade away.

In the meantime, however, the close URL naming with only the .com vs. .net to differentiate the two, caused a lot of confusion among prospective advertisers. The .net operation was haphazard and tough to navigate through. This created negative word-of-mouth that crossed over to the .com operation and made selling ad space on the Provincetown.com Web site that much more difficult.

Other Web site competitors operated out of Hyannis, Edgartown, and Dennis—all major tourist destinations on Cape Cod that were located closer to Boston. Provincetown was on the tip of the Cape and required an extra 45–60 minutes to get to once a visitor reached the "tonier" towns of Hyannis and Edgartown. Skip believed this geographical isolation had kept central Cape Web site owners from poaching into his geographic territory. On the other hand, Skip believed he needed to grow out of Provincetown and begin to attract businesses from the entire "elbow" of the Cape. From there, Skip wanted to expand westward eventually to Hyannis. This move, however, would be a huge leap for his Web site operation and would remain some years away assuming Provincetown.com was successful.

The "Product"

The Web site's home page could be easily accessed using the address www.Provincetown.com. The Internet user then had choices among entertainment, commercial street, village, and general information interfaces (see Figure 1 for hard copy visuals of several Web site pages). Subsequently, this led to subdirectories providing visitors with information along the commercial street to "where to stay," "retail shops," "restaurants," "real estate," and "services."

Potential and existing advertisers perceived the site as another way of attracting business that they might not ordinarily get if they did not have a presence on the Internet. Besides carrying advertising copy and visuals, Provincetown.com also provided these other services:

- Hosting a site as a subdomain
- Obtaining domain names for clients
- Designing Web pages
- Acting as marketing agents for clients to get them listings in other Internet locations
- Offering priority placement within certain Web pages
- Establishing "easy update" systems whereby advertisers, once specially trained, could go into their Web page and change text or pictures on their own without having to go through Doug. This was very helpful to real estate agents.
- Uploading material, such as local Provincetown newspapers, which put news material each week on the site.

Keeping up the Web site with the latest events occurring in Provincetown, listing new advertisers, de-listing those that dropped out, designing new sites, and redesigning old ones was a full-time job for Doug. "I am committing to making our site the best on the Cape," he mentioned. "My design, communication, and coding skills along with an energetic imagination made me capable of inventing original, yet intuitive, tools and processes that browsers of our Web site can understand and use comfortably."

Pricing

Each Web page within the Provincetown.com domain carried only one advertiser. The ad space allocated by Doug for the advertising was a block of space along the left-hand side of each Web page. No actual limit existed on the total size of the advertisement because the viewer could just keep scrolling down the page. Promotional copy could run through several screens of information on a single Web page if the advertiser wanted it to. The home page was considered the most valuable space; for this, Seaman's Bank paid $2,500 for the 1999 calendar year.

Pricing for other advertisers depended upon their placement within the Web site and what Skip and Doug felt they could charge the client for their advertising message. "It's still a fairly new world out there," Skip was saying. "We don't have rate cards like television and radio stations do. We're still making it up as we go along. With more experience under our belts, we'll be able to standardize how we charge for advertising in perhaps one or two years."

Promotion

The team at Provincetown.com had a two-tier task when it came to promoting the Web site. They had to sell themselves to advertisers; they also had to attract Internet browsers to their URL.

Speaking to this point, the marketing director said, "When I approach a prospective advertiser, I'm prepared for them to say, 'Why do I need the Internet?' Some of the more sophisticated clients challenge me with, 'I already have my own home page. Why do I need you?'"

In answer to these questions, the team responded with the following list of "reasons why" potential advertisers should seriously consider taking space on the site:

1. Provincetown.com had a high awareness factor. People were looking to the Web site to provide needed information and facts.

2. High awareness = high exposure. Those commercial businesses that looked for the tourist dollar could count on Provincetown.com to provide incremental inquiries and business.

3. The Web site had achieved "critical mass." It was an accepted and trusted media outlet and source for reliable information. People counted on the site to rely data both to and from advertisers and prospective visitors to the area.

4. Even if the advertiser had his/her own Web page, a linkage with Provincetown.com would prove to be very advantageous. Not linked to the Web site could mean serious potential loss of business to those commercial enterprises that had already linked up.

Skip said, "The saying, 'You snooze, you lose,' is what we are attempting to convey to all of the commercial interests in the Provincetown area. If you feel you have to be in the newspaper or on cable or on the radio to get your message across, then we believe you have to be visible on the Provincetown.com Web site, too. More and more people around the world are planning their vacations or conducting business or even shopping using their office or home computer. Any businessperson who doesn't realize this will lose out. The whole nature of communications and the way we do business, especially retailing, is changing rapidly and it will be forever changed.

"Either you get on the bandwagon now or you're going to be left behind. And I'd hate to be the guy left behind. Because it's business suicide not to be up there with everyone else."

The other issue for the Web site was to build its audience—the number of "hits" it received daily and the total "unique visitors." To do that, Skip and Doug advertised their URL in local and Boston newspapers and small, targeted seasonal (summer) magazines. The URL was cross-listed in approximately 2,000 other Web sites, but given the proliferation of URLs, Provincetown.com was still too easy to miss as a computer user.

Target Audiences

The Web site had multiple target audiences, but two in particular were going to be critical for the Web site's success. The first audience was the local community. Provincetown for years had been home to, and was accepting towards, gays as well as to the heterosexual community. The overall atmosphere in the Provincetown area was one of acceptance of alternative lifestyles and living arrangements.

The second key audience was the seasonal tourist "invasion" from April to October. These were the "make-it-or-break-it" months for the retail stores, restaurants, and motels in Provincetown. Typically, the November to March period was very quiet with a good number of the local people wintering in Florida or other sunny climes.

Skip believed the Web site had to appeal to both groups without seeming to favor one over the other. It was a "fine line," as he referred to it, but one he felt was extremely important to observe and be sensitive towards.

The Marketing Problem

Skip was facing what he felt were several crucial decisions regarding the Provincetown.com Web site. First, he had only been involved part-time up until now while Doug was full-time. Should he jump in? What could he bring to the table that could really propel the URL into profitability?

Another concern was how to grow the site. In which direction should the management team focus their efforts? Expand the Web site geographically? Segment the business community in Provincetown more finely to achieve more penetration? Change their pricing? Explore ecommerce? Additionally, there were real problems regarding the Web site's acceptance of credit card payments. Did Skip really want to expose his fledgling business to such problems?

Although Skip and Doug had increased the number of daily unique visitors coming to the Web site, compared to other successful commercial sites they still had a long way to go. Skip figured a goal of 25,000 visitors per day would make the Web site much more attractive to potential advertisers, hence getting him closer to financial viability. If Provincetown.com were already cross-listed with 2,000 other Web sites, what more could he do to create site awareness? What should the management team do to ramp up the site's "hits"?

Make vs. Buy

Would owning and hosting his own domain through a server, instead of renting the services from an ISP, save money and/or create more revenue? Could this be quantified? Would that also help Skip carry out credit card transactions more securely?

Finances

Skip listed his annual expenses to operate the Web site:

Employee salaries	$ 55,000
Internet Service Provider fee	25,000
Office rent	8,000
Utilities (telephone, electricity)	4,000
Advertising	4,000
Miscellaneous	4,000
Total:	$ 100,000

This amount did not include paying Skip back for his initial up-front investment of $50,000 to the previous owner of the Provincetown.com Web site. Ideally, he wanted that sum paid back within five years.

Skip then considered the revenue side of the business. His best estimate for the year was as follows:

Advertising space on the Web site	$ 65,000
Designing Web pages	17,500
Other services	15,000
Total:	$ 97,500

True, it was not break-even but Skip felt that at least he was covering most of his out-of-pocket costs for operating the Web site. He wondered if he could charge a commission on the sales that accrued to the businesses through his Web site. In that case, how was he going to prove that the sales originated at Provincetown.com?

Figure 1. Provincetown.com Web Site Visuals

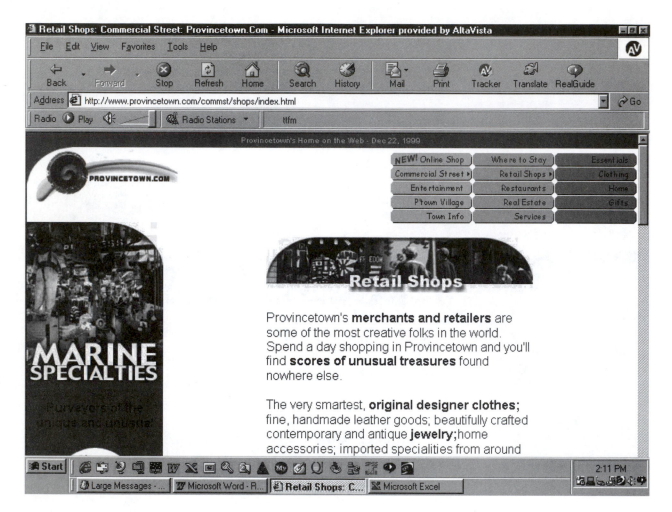

Figure 1. Provincetown.com Web Site Visuals *(continued)*

Case 9.2
Innovative Therapists International[*]

Introduction

Phil Johnson felt he was pulled in so many directions at once, he didn't know which fire to put out first. "I may be the CEO of Innovative Therapists International (ITI) here in Tucson, but I feel more like I'm the proverbial 'chief bottle washer' with responsibilities spread all over the United States. Every day I have to make purchasing, manufacturing, sales, marketing, publicity, general management, accounting, financial, human resources, and systems decisions. It can drive me nuts. But truthfully, there's nothing else I'd rather be doing."

Background

Phil is married to, and partnered in business with, Sara Rosenfeld-Johnson, a brilliant and sought after speech and language pathologist who has developed breakthrough techniques in her field of oral-motor therapy. Sara, with degrees from Ithaca College and Columbia University, has 25-years experience in physiologically-based speech and language disorders specializing in pre-school and school-aged children.

Phil retired from high school teaching in 1994 after working with both typical and special needs children for 25 years. He saw the way his wife, Sara, was expanding her therapy consulting practice and believed he could be more productive working with her than continuing as a teacher. "I thought it would be pretty easy to learn-as-you-go as the business expanded. Wow, was I wrong. It's been a challenge and a half."

How It All Began

Sara had built up her therapy practice both in Westchester County, New York, and adjoining Fairfield County, Connecticut, so much that by 1992 she could easily have worked 80–100 hours per week and still not have satisfied the demand from parents for her to treat their children. As a speech and language pathologist, Sara worked extensively with a pediatric population by helping young children overcome speech clarity and eating problems caused by birth defects, illness, and/or injuries.

Her innovative techniques, which at times she referred to as "physical therapy for the mouth," included generating ideas for products that she and other therapists could use to help children and adults overcome their oral-motor deficiencies. As her reputation grew, so did demand for Sara's services. She hated to turn away any parent who called her for advice, counsel, and/or therapy for their child, but Sara had also reached her physical and emotional limits in 1991.

---

[*] Some of the names are disguised.

There was one other problem. Sara felt she could provide more good for more people in the long run by *teaching* other therapists how to provide the same kind of articulation and feeding programs she had been undertaking the past two decades. Instead of working alone, Sara wanted to extend her knowledge base to hundreds, if not thousands, of other therapists working in the United States and around the world with special needs children.

The question she repeatedly asked herself was how could she do this?

Starting the Clinic

The answer, after Sara and Phil considered a lot of different business relationships and options, was the Sara R. Johnson Oral-Motor Speech and Language Associates Clinic that was established in 1992 in South Salem, New York. Here, Sara was able to recruit, train, and supervise the efforts of several dozen full- and part-time speech pathologists who were able to serve a much broader-based population in age and geographic dispersion than Sara had ever been able to achieve while working alone.

About this time, Sara and Phil Johnson decided to move their family to Tucson for personal reasons, including giving Sara the opportunity to explore her interests in teaching. Sara hired Toni Kline, a speech pathologist like herself, to become director of the South Salem, New York, clinic.

Speaking Tours

As part of her education effort, Sara decided to begin speaking to groups of speech pathologists, physical therapists, occupational therapists, special education teachers, and parents all across the nation. For the first year, Sara became part of a speaker's bureau that handled all aspects of Sara's seminars for an agreed-upon stipend regardless of the size of the audience. With this experience under her belt, Sara believed she could produce and market her own seminars as part of the clinic's offerings. It was at this point that Phil retired from teaching and began the business partnership with his wife.

Videotapes

Under the clinic's auspices, Sara and Phil began to develop treatment plans for oral-motor therapy on videotape that therapists could purchase to learn Sara's approach without having to meet and train with Sara directly. The therapy showed fellow speech pathologists how to work with children and adults in the development of the muscles of the mouth needed for speech clarity and for eating.

Therapy Tools

Sara began to use a variety of items and toys that would further facilitate her approach to oral-motor therapy. The major items included a wide array of horns, straws, and bubble-blowing equipment all designed to improve oral-motor development while facilitating speech clarity. The entire contents of Sara and Toni Kline's oral-motor, feeding, and sensory kits are shown as Figure 1.

ITI Is Spun Off

It was at this point in 1997 that the videotape production, tool therapy manufacture, and marketing of Sara's speaking tours were spun off financially from the clinic and a new company was incorporated: Innovative Therapists International or "ITI." Phil became the company's CEO. The company started to publish a catalog that now included Sara's book, *Oral-Motor Exercises for Speech Clarity*, first made available in mid-1999; videotapes; therapy tools; and Sara's schedule of speaking engagements. In 1998, the company paid for the development of its own Web site, www.oromotorsp.com (see Figure 2).

Phenomenal Growth

Phil perceived the organization as a continuing education company that would provide texts and supplies to augment and complement the therapies that Sara would teach in her seminars. Growth had been nothing short of phenomenal from 1995 to 1999 and Phil now had five part-time staff people working for him to keep up with orders.

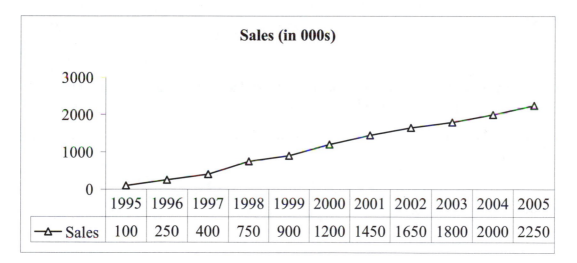

Sales (in 000s)

Sales	1995	1996	1997	1998	1999	2000	2001	2002	2003	2004	2005
Sales	100	250	400	750	900	1200	1450	1650	1800	2000	2250

Note: Sales for years 1995–1998 are actual; 1999–2005 are estimated

The Environment for ITI

The competition for attendance at medical and health seminars, workshops, and conferences was fierce. Because such presentations could be very rewarding financially, literally dozens of speakers offered their services in the United States on how best to provide oral-motor and speech therapies. The challenge for Sara and Phil was to obtain "their share of the conference pie."

A further challenge to ITI was that independent therapists and those hired by school systems and hospitals had only limited funds to attend educational programs designed to enhance their skills.

Attendees had to pick and choose a conference or workshop carefully because they might be able to go to one, perhaps two, each year. Therapists, therefore, were attracted to those presentations from "known" or "hot" speakers who had received solid word-of-mouth recommendations from other professionals in their field.

Time away from the job was another factor to consider. Creating open days in busy therapy calendars was difficult enough; for independent therapists in their own private practices, it meant foregoing income. Conference and workshop information had to be delivered efficiently, clearly, and "painlessly" to an audience that often wanted immediate solutions to very tough therapy problems in a limited one- or two-day time frame.

The Two-Tier Series

Sara developed a two-tier workshop series in response to therapists' learning needs while at the same time being aware of the limited time they could be away from the job. Fees listed below only reflect the cost of attending the workshop; travel, hotel, and food expenses were extra.

65% of all attendees:

Level 1:

- A two-day workshop with Sara that outlined her "Three-Part Treatment Plan for Oral-Motor Therapy." Cost: $230 per person. 6 hours per day. Average attendance: 65.

- A one-day workshop with Toni Kline for a presentation on feeding. Cost: $130. 6 hours per day. Average attendance: 80.

35% of all attendees:

Level 2 (Prerequisite: attendance at Level 1 training):

- A two-day advanced workshop with Sara teaching diagnostic and program planning. Cost: $230. 6 hours per day. Average attendance: 35.

- A two-day workshop with Toni Kline for a presentation on feeding. Cost: $230. 6 hours per day. Average attendance: 50.

Mailings

In order to generate these attendance rates, Phil oversaw the mailing of some 4,000 brochures promoting each of Sara's programs to therapists who practiced in and around the city chosen for the five-day program. Often, however, Phil would find out that a sizeable number of the therapists who signed up for one of the programs had never received a brochure at all, but had come to the conference through word-of-mouth mentions from other therapists who had previously attended one or more of Sara's conferences. The mailing lists Phil used had been purchased from the American Speech and Hearing Association (ASHA), the national accrediting association for speech pathologists in the United States. Possibly, there were problems with the lists since each mailing of 4,000 brochures netted only about 1% in actual conference attendees. Phil theorized either the lists were incomplete, out of date, or inaccurate or a combination of the three. Phil promised himself to investigate this further at some point.

Attendee Reactions

Reaction sheets given to attendees at the end of each workshop confirmed what Sara intuitively knew during each day's presentation: therapists, special education teachers, and parents for the most part all felt Sara's approach to oral-motor development was excellent. A good number of attendees even wrote the workshops were the best they had ever been to. Sara had a "good news, bad news" reaction to the positive comments. "I have a really good concept on how to help people with speech clarity and eating problems," she was saying, "but even with all our efforts to publicize ITI, the vast majority of therapists have never heard of us. Phil estimated only 8% of registered speech pathologists knew about me. How do we reach the other 92%?"

Positioning

Sara decided to differentiate herself from other therapist-speakers by emphasizing technique over theory and putting together an entire package of materials including a handbook, catalog, videotape series, individual therapy products and kits, and a Web site. In addition, anyone attending one of her workshops was offered the opportunity to e-mail Sara where s/he could present Sara with a particularly thorny therapy problem for which they wished a consultation.

This seemed to be working. By summer 1999 Sara was averaging about 30–35 e-mails a day to answer as follow-ups to the workshops she gave. Fellow therapists were apparently reacting very positively about this one-on-one opportunity to communicate with Sara.

Sites

For 1999, Sara was speaking at these ITI workshop locations:

January	Austin, Texas
February	Scottsdale, Arizona
March	Woodland and Monterey, California
April	Asheville, North Carolina; Stockton, California
July	Boston and New York City
August	Rochester, New York; Chicago, Illinois; Sacramento, California
September	Baltimore
October	Portland, Oregon; Philadelphia
November	Ft. Lauderdale, Florida; Monterey, California
December	Mountainside, New Jersey

The goal eventually was for Sara to speak on average twice each month and expand her geographical base eventually to North America, Latin America, Europe, and Israel.

Pressures

The breakneck pace resulting from the success of their ITI venture was starting to take its toll. Sara was allocating more and more of her time to e-mailing therapists; preparing presentations; keeping in touch with the clinic by phone, fax and e-mail while visiting the clinic in person 3–4 times a year; and developing new therapy tools for the catalog.

Phil was concentrating on the financial, production, and marketing aspects of the operation. He felt he was barely keeping his head above water. "I wish there were ways I could improve my efficiency. I've gotten much better at marketing the seminars in each of our key cities and we are building attendance everywhere Sara goes. But I'm frustrated about two things: how low awareness levels are among the therapy community about our company, ITI, and Sara in particular, and also, how little business we are getting from our Web site. It cost a lot to set up and maintain, but only 5% of our revenues are generated through the Internet. That's very disappointing and something I hope we can improve."

Figure 1. Feeding Aids

12

Feeding

Feeding Aids

We have chosen a number of our favorite feeding aids to share with you. Each item is proven to minimize sensory defensiveness and enhance a client's oral-motor skills. You will find the diversity and utility of these tools to be invaluable to your therapeutic feeding programs.

Latex Super Gloves are a "must have" for all oral-motor therapy programs. Be sure to wear them "tight" to achieve the natural sensation clients prefer. Three sizes are available in boxes of 100 each. Or choose our popular, kid-friendly flavored gloves. Vinyl Super Gloves are also available.

Latex Super Gloves - Item LSG - Box of 100 (specify XS, S or M)
Flavored gloves - Box of 100 (specify XS, S or M)
   Strawberry - Item LGS
   Bubble gum - Item LGB
Vinyl Super Gloves (used only for clients with diagnosed latex intolerance) - Item VSG - Box of 100 (specify S or M)

1. **The Honey Bear with Straw** is proven effective with children as young as 8 months. The Honey Bear allows you to control the flow of liquid into a child's mouth and encourages children to learn how to straw drink. You will also appreciate the spill-proof lid.

   Item HB

2. **The Sit 'n Sip Self-Feeding Bottle Straw** helps reduce the risk of ear infection by encouraging a child to drink in an upright position. Sit 'n Sip also assists in the transition to cup drinking.

   Item SSB

Thick-It is the answer for clients who have trouble swallowing thin liquids. Available in two concentrations to meet your specific needs. 6 per pack.

Item T1 - Original .28 oz
Item T2 - Concentrated .16 oz

Figure 1. Feeding Aids *(continued)*

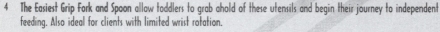

Feeding Aids

1 **Maroon Spoons** are available in two functional sizes. These colorful spoons make mealtime fun while promoting optimal oral movement and lip closure.

Items SMS (1-inch bowl), & LMS (1.25-inch bowl)

2 **The Soft Flex Spoon** is made of soft plastic. This convenient tool features two spoons in one. Ideal for tender gums.

Item SFS

3 **The Soft Bite Spoon** is covered with a soft plastic coating for protection. This handy spoon is perfect to use with teething babies.

Item SBS

4 **The Easiest Grip Fork and Spoon** allow toddlers to grab ahold of these utensils and begin their journey to independent feeding. Also ideal for clients with limited wrist rotation.

Item FS

5 The **MagMag Straw Cup** helps kids to learn to drink independently and this cup with no-spill top gets things started. Independent straw drinking helps develop jaw stability, lip rounding, and tongue retraction.

Item MTS

6 The **MagMag Drinking Cup** allows you to take independent drinking one step further. This wide-rimmed, spill-proof cup promotes transitioning from bottle to cup drinking. The functional handles also keep hands at midline.

Item MMC

7 With the **Infa Trainer Cup**, you can adjust the flow of this multifaceted cup, and its wide, open lid allows for stability without encouraging a suckle.

Item ITC

8 **Cut-out Cups** are available in pink (1 oz.) and blue (2 oz.). Flexible Cut-out Cups stimulate the corners of the mouth to facilitate lip closure and allow a child to drink without head/neck extension.

Item PC (pink)
Item BC (blue)

Oral Motor Therapy Home Page   Page 1 of 2

ORAL - MOTOR
SPEECH THERAPY

INNOVATIVE
THERAPISTS
INTERNATIONAL

TUCSON • ARIZONA

ARE YOU FRUSTRATED WITH THOSE DIFFICULT TO
CORRECT ARTICULATION PROBLEMS? HERE'S YOUR
ANSWER. COMBINE TRADITIONAL SPEECH THERAPY WITH
THE NEW, INNOVATIVE AND HIGHLY SUCCESSFUL ORAL-
MOTOR SPEECH THERAPY.

Innovative Therapist is a Continuing Education Company designed to provide the very
best workshops to help Therapists learn the "fun", "practical" and very "effective"
techniques associated with Oral-Motor Therapy.

Sara R. Johnson, M.S., CCC/SLP, has developed easy to use techniques for diagnosing
and treating clients with oral-motor/feeding/speech disorders in clients of all ages and
ability levels.

For More Information		
**Product Catalog**	_**Conference Content**_	_**Speaker Bio's**_
**Mission Statement**	_**Conference Dates**_	_**Visit Our Clinic**_
**Articles about Oral-Motor Therapy**		
**Fill out ITI's 2 minute questionnaire**		

Correspondance and Ordering Information

Innovative Therapists International

Innovative Therapists International / info@oromotorsp.com
Privacy Statement

Site maintained by:

http://www.oromotorsp.com/   01/05/2000

Figure 2. Web Site

Innovative Therapists International
Product Catalog

❖Index❖

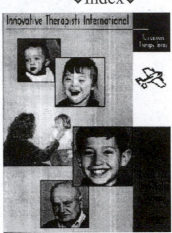

Oral-Motor Kits
Feeding Aids
Exercise Supplies
Sensory Items
Books
Videos
Miscellaneous
   Individual Straws
   Individual Horns
   Evaluation Forms

Home

Use the section to the left to see the catalog items.
Print an order form

Home

Fill out ITI's 2 minute questionnaire

Figure 2. Web Site *(continued)*